A Heavenly Hook Up

Proof that God will be as involved in our relationships as we let Him

DeWayne M. Thomas

A Heavenly Hook Up

DeWayne M. Thomas

Cover concept and design by

Copyright © 2014

PUBLISHED BY:
BRENTWOOD CHRISTIAN PRESS
WWW.BRENTWOODBOOKS.COM
COLUMBUS, GEORGIA 31904

Acknowledgements

Special thanks to those who helped us with editing, Sister Chante Thomas Hood and and Sister Zakkyya Williams.

Thanks to those who have imparted encouragement and wisdom into us: My mom, Ms Evelyn "Chief" Thomas, Jacqui's mom, Mrs. Jimmie Thompson and our pastors: Bishop A. Livingston Foxworth, Pastor Nelson Taylor, and Bishop Demetrius Roscoe.

I also want to give special thanks and honor to my wife, Mrs Jacqualine Thomas

Preface

Our eyes filled with excitement and anticipation. Our minds like little nets. There we sat, waiting to catch the next words that would drop from my great grandmother's lips, Mrs. Maggie Harris. Raising her age-softened voice to mimic the chicken hawk's voice, "'I make my living by vain.' He flapped his wings to stay aloft as he boasted to the buzzard. The buzzard, with outstretched wings soaring on the air replied, "'I just wait on the salvation of the Lord.' The chicken hawk responded, 'Do you see those chickens down there? Just watch me. I can catch two at a time.'" Raising and lowering her hands to demonstrate the flap of the chicken hawk, she continued, "The hawk swooped down and caught two chickens, one in each claw." As she sat we encircled her feet. I could not stand not knowing how big the chicken hawk was. What did it look like? I thought. I had to ask. As I raised my hand, my cousin pushed my hand down to stop me. "Let her finish the story," he whispered. Gran-ma went on sharing, "Now while the chicken hawk was boasting that he made his living by vain, a sly fox had been watching and listening to everything… and waiting.. As soon as the chicken hawk made its way outside the chicken coop, flying very low because of the load, he met his fate. Just when the hawk was at the right height, that old sly fox climbed atop the coop then jumped into the air and killed the chicken hawk and took the chickens! 'Well Sir,' said the buzzard flying high up in the sky circling the dead chicken hawk, 'It is just like I said. I wait on the salvation of the Loooord!'" At the end of her telling the fable of course, the questions would come. Yes, just a flood of questions from us listeners. It was during these times that I can remember feeling a kind of safeness only found in the love of close bonds created when life's leisures weren't so crowded by technology.

Telling stories and yarns has been a tradition in our family for as long—well, I guess as long as we have been around. I suppose I have spent my fair share of time spinning a good yarn or two. Some of us might call them anecdotes or jokes, but for sentimental reasons I like to refer to them as yarns. I suppose it was out of that tradition that I unwittingly received my first opportunities, as a child, to share tales of the simple life on the hilltop in Teaspoon, Florida. However, what I have been given to share in this book is not a yarn, but a true-life account of God's divine interest in the relationships of His people. There are more tales that perhaps opportunity would allow me to share at another time, but this story might be one of the most important I've ever been given to share. Some of the happenings you read in this book may lead you to think it just another yarn. I thought about omitting some of the more strange occurrences. Consider this, if I deleted all of the many inexplicable occurrences, referred only to what is considered rational, and deliberately omitted the invasions of the natural by the supernatural, what I'm about to share with you might be more plausible. But if I did that, it would not be the truth. Besides, in doing so, there are those who might say I would be stealing glory from God Himself.

The events of my life are reminiscent of the folktale, Brer Rabbit and the Tar Baby. Why, you ask? To put it simply, the more I put my hands on the situation to fix it, the more entangled my situation became. As a child, folks would often warn me to leave whatever my mind and hands had found alone, and they warned me not to be so hard-headed. You would think I'd listen better, especially after the fire that nearly ended my life. I spent most of my very young years in the company of our family's patriarchs and matriarchs; I suppose had I been able to keep their wise words, my life would have been very different. Please do not misunderstand me, I really did try but sometimes I would find myself in over my head.

Well my friend (I hope I can call you friend) you are still reading so at this juncture that would make us friends. Sometimes you need supernatural help. This story reveals the necessity for God to intervene. The unique way, time, and events that brought my wife, Jacqui, and I together could only have been orchestrated by God. I'm sure you will agree as you read our story. This book is an account of how God brought the wife of my destiny to me. The events that were to take place during that time in my life would be the inspiration from which this book is written. I invite you to immerse your thoughts and imagination as each chapter guides you to a better place in faith, hope and love.

Table of Contents

Chapter 1:
A House is Not a Home When Nothing's There

It was a Wednesday evening, in late January 1988. I was finishing a long day assisting Colonel Oliver Boyd who we affectionately called Col. OBD, short for One Bad Dude, as he was a real icon around the center. It was nothing for him to see sixty dental patients in one day, and I was pleased to be a part of his legacy. He gave me a lift home that afternoon. My wife Carol, her sons, from her previous marriage, and I had moved into a three-bedroom home due to the impending birth of our son, DeWayne Junior (DJ). We were happy to move and had only resided at our new address for a short while. So short in fact, I had not really learned the actual address and only knew where it was by sight.

The colonel let me out at the corner. As I approached our home I noticed that our good car, an '86 Montego, was not in the driveway and wondered to myself where Carol and the kids could be this late in the day. Trash and paper were curiously strewn about the yard. The boys' bikes were gone. Becoming anxious, I stepped up the pace of my approach. When I reached the house the door was ajar. As I entered, I was completely stunned. Nothing could have prepared me for what I saw in front of me. The entire place was empty. My mind raced with a flood of questions as beads of sweat gathered on my forehead. I ran from room to room calling out to my absent family. "Carol!" I called frantically, but there was no answer. Finally conceding to the reality that they were no longer there, I needed an explanation. In an attempt to seek answers I went to my neighbor's home to ask if they had seen anything suspicious. I don't know why I asked, people were always moving in and out of base housing, but at that point I was plain old desperate. As I stood in the doorway talking to my neighbor, I noticed our newly restored antique dining room table in the back-ground. There it was, as plain as day sitting in their house, in their dining room no less. I could not help asking how they had come by it. Michelle quickly let me know that Carol had sold it to her earlier. With trepidation, I asked how much she had sold it for. Having done the restoration, I knew the mahogany was inlaid with beryl and worth well over $1,500. My neighbor nonchalantly replied, "$100." My chest tightened as though suddenly gripped by a vice. I don't know why I was so fixated on the table. Maybe it was the visible display that represented the loss of ownership and accomplishment. This table was an evident display of the abrupt interruption of my hopes and dreams. I could sense the feeling of fear and rage gathering at my mind's gate. I struggled to hold on to what little civility that remained. I could hear my mind saying, You need to move on. To my chagrin, I complied by changing the subject and asked if she had observed the name of the moving company. She replied, "A few guys and a U-Haul helped your wife move out." Incensed and speechless, I calmly stepped back out of their entrance way and returned to the empty cave that remained next door. I wanted to take an inventory of what remained. The haze of fear and anger clouded my mind, and entering into the emptiness of each room sent chills to my core. My body began to quake as I wondered through the house several times and finally sat down on the things that were left behind. A few suits and a pile of uni-forms sat in the center of what used to be our living room.

As I walked over to it, I collapsed there in a heap. After a few minutes of crying and mulling the situation over in my head, I conducted a mental account. There was no bed to sleep in, no pillow to lay my head on, my rings, pictures and other personal items were gone. I was not sure if she actually thought about these items as they moved the furniture out, or if she randomly picked over my belongings without intent. Only my military stuff remained, along with some odds and end food items. I don't know how to express the emptiness I felt. Images of the boys running up the stairs to claim their bedrooms when we moved in filled my mind. The walls littered with picture wire and holders, the floor still shining from the new tile— the entire affair was surreal. I thought for a moment, maybe I should call someone, but at the time, no one came to mind. I found myself sifting through the trash strewn about the floor looking for some pictures of DJ, but that was a lost cause. As a family we did not use the camera often, so pictures were sparse at best. After digging around unsuccessfully, I sat down. I soon drifted off to sleep hoping that when I awoke this nightmare would be over.

When I woke up the next morning with hopes of looking over to see Carol, everything was still the same. The aching sensation in the pit of my stomach and the sting that overtook my heart the day before quickly returned. I pondered the irony of my aspirations to rescue someone upon entering this relationship. I thought I would be the difference for her and her sons as she exited her previous marriage. In fact this wasn't the first time she left me—the first time, she left while she was pregnant with DJ. Had I not been in rescue-mode then, our marriage would have already ended in divorce. However, now I found myself needing to be rescued. My life was a wreck and I needed a Holy Ghost hook up and tow out of this pit.

After showering and changing my uniform I felt the intense urge to run. I was surprised as I was not an avid runner. I suppose, I should not have been surprised, especially since God's M.O. is to use simple things to confound the wise. It was almost as if I was compelled to run. I didn't care where; I just wanted to run somewhere. I lived approximately two and a half miles from my work center—so I ran. I ran effortlessly without sweat or even breathing hard. This was odd. I mean, I could run but I wasn't that good. To do this it was apparent, not only had God spoken to me, but also he had supernaturally aided me. As I ran, the Lord began to audibly speak to me about my situation. At first I was frightened. I thought I was losing my mind. But something inside me whispered, "This is God. Listen." It was then that things became pretty intense. He said, "My son I am with you. I have seen your efforts and know your heart. I will return your son to you. I will restore your household. It shall be seven times greater than before. I am the Lord God; I will give you the wife that I have prepared for you. I will provide all your needs." I could hear this repeating in my spirit over and over again. I suppose a lot happened in those fifteen minutes, but the most important thing was I knew without a doubt that God the Father was with me. He had inspired me to run and from this encounter I had peace. He had spoken to me and assured me that He was working everything out. I could barely contain the joy that was within my soul. I cried and sang with all that was in me. I suppose some onlookers thought my behavior odd. It mattered not; I wanted to bless the Lord.

As I approached the dental center I noticed my supervisor leaning out of the rear entrance. When I reached the door she said something that confirmed all that God had said to me, "The Lord spoke to me in a dream last night and told me you would need to take the day off to attend to some urgent personal matters, and that you would need my car to do it. So here are the keys to my car. Just bring it back this evening." She said it so matter-of-factly that I didn't hesitate. I took the keys and scurried off to her car. Where should I go first? I thought, as I tried to slow down the flurry of emotions that were pressing my soul. The first face that came to my mind was my friend and pastor, Dr. Neil Peterson. Now, it is important that you know that Dr. Peterson was also a practicing lawyer. He was a logical man whose thought processes, though protracted at times, were always lucent and wise. I was fortunate that he was my pastor. I went to him to seek advice and counsel and shared with him what had occurred earlier, and how God promised he would deliver my son to me. Dr. Peterson's reply was a bit surprising considering he was a pastor. He however, was speaking as a lawyer and in no uncertain terms pronounced, " Son, at this time, for a man to receive custody of a child in the state of Mississippi, the child's mother would have to abandon the child on top of a telephone pole." Hearing this, I paused for a moment and stated, "I guess that is what will have to happen because the Lord has promised, and I know His word is true." I then asked if he could help me with my divorce. He replied, "Brother DeWayne, I cannot help you because I am a pastor to the both of you." I replied, "I understand, thank you." As I stood up and headed towards the door, he summoned me back scribbling on the back his business card, "I have a friend who might be able to help you." He handed me the lawyer's name. "Tell him I sent you". I departed and immediately called the recommended lawyer. While I conveyed the situation to the lawyer, my thoughts began to fixate on where Carol and the kids might be when I remembered that DJ had a doctor's appointment that day. I knew that I only needed to follow Carol when she left the doctor's office to find out where they were staying. I swiftly made my way over to the clinic and sure enough she was there and on her way out to the car. Being careful not to be seen, I followed her — out of Biloxi, Mississippi, over the Back Bay Bridge, weaving through traffic,barely beating stop lights until we finally arrived at their apartment complex. Relieved that I knew where my son was, I thought it best to do nothing immediately. And seeing that I was borrowing my supervisor's car, it was paramount that I look after it. After all, I wasn't sure where things might lead if I confronted Carol head on. I sat there for a few minutes hoping that I might catch a glimpse of DJ, and after an unsuccessful wait I decided to leave.

Later that evening I returned the car to my supervisor. To express my appreciation I offered to have dinner with her. As we sat at the table across from each other in an awkward silence, our emotions were palpable. My supervisor and impromptu confidante understood my sorrow and wanted to comfort me but she dare not, and nor could I let her. I was too vulnerable. In my mind I knew it could lead to a costly misstep. In my spirit I heard, Leave now. God knew that this kindness could have easily been corrupted. Knowing this, we quickly parted with her driving me home, where I found myself alone again. There, I began to think.

If there ever was a time for a brother to have a pity party, I felt entirely justified. There I was without anything except a few discarded items, my uniforms and a dead car in the driveway. I had not really thought much about overcoming the earlier temptation with my supervisor. Our obedience was far better than sacrificing it all foolishly, for a few moments of pleasure. I soon felt the emptiness of the house and I knew I needed help to make it through the night. The only thing I could think to do was pray. While praying for a means of transportation and custody of my son, I was inspired to do something that was very strange regarding the old Ford that had died a while back and now was occupying space in the driveway. It had a cracked block that made it inoperable. Once again God interrupted my natural course with step-by-step supernatural instructions: I was to take Carol's ceramic casting slip (used to pour ceramic figures) and pour it into the radiator of the dead car, then gather some of her HerbaLife and diet supplement pills, mix it with water and pour the mixture into the radiator. After I did this I was to rev the engine as high as I could for about fifteen minutes. I had no idea why or what I was doing. It was scary. As I revved the engine the street was filled with white and blue smoke along with noxious exhaust fumes. The muffler was cracked and the noise from the engine was loud and obtrusive. Neighbors nervously peeped through their doors and windows as they investigated the commotion. Nevertheless, I persisted in revving the engine. The exhaust manifold glowed red hot, the radiator started to hiss, then suddenly the white smoke stopped and the engine ran smooth. The Lord then said to let it cool for about an hour. I waited and then poured water in the radiator and it did not leak. It was a miracle!! You see, earlier in the week I had tried putting fluid into the car and as fast as I poured it in, it would leak out through the crack in the engine block. Well now, with my second transportation hook up of the day, I knew God was on my side and I started to feel my oats! I just knew God wanted me to go get my son. I felt God wanted me to go and do something. Although I did not hear God say anything of the sort, I just knew he wanted me to go get him.

I jumped in the car and hurried over to the apartment where I had learned Carol was staying with the kids. When I arrived, I knocked hastily at the door. Carol did not respond and proceeded to turn out every light in the apartment. During this little episode I was wrestling with the Lord who was actually telling me not to go there. He said to leave the apartments and to trust in Him. I finally submitted to God's will and returned to my car and started down street. Just then, the police drove up and almost saw me! Whew! Had I been seen it would have been one more thing to answer for—I could have been arrested. That would have been real nice for the devil. My impatience almost jeopardized what I knew to be true and would have created a real mess. I guess I was adding to God's instructions out of my own emotions. Here God had provided the Holy Ghost hook up that I needed, but the whirlwind of events caused me to almost miss the miracle. I had not yet learned to completely surrender to God, to be obedient to His instructions and not be led by feelings, as you may know it can be very difficult.

Chapter 2:
God Hitched

The calamity that had just rained on my life pressed me to take time off from work. I drove home to Century, Florida to visit with my family and share with them the most recent happenings in my life. The short retreat to the country rejuvenated me and I felt strong enough to return to work. My heart had been made ready to try following the Word of God to the best of my ability. Now humbled, I concluded that the entire downward-spiraling episode of my life was my fault.

I accepted the blame for it all. The choices that I made were contrary to the will of God and had been all along. It was I who had started the whole thing by initiating a relationship that I knew was contrary to the will and Word of God. It was I who believed that I could change a circumstance that was beyond my control. It was I who tried to be someone else's savior instead fully trusting the Lordship of Christ. These realizations lead me down the path of restoration. I started spending as much time as possible praying and seeking godly counsel. I began witnessing to the lost and teaching the uncompromising Word of God to those who would listen.

I will never forget, the nights of preaching people from drunkeness to sobriety and salvation, right there on Division Street in Biloxi, MS Talk about irony; nearly two years earlier I was among those who were partying and living for themselves. Thank God for his mercy and grace! On Friday and Saturday nights the Baptist Church would have street services and they allowed me to join in with them. It was great taking turns preaching the Word of God to the lost souls. Acknowledging the source of my success, I elected to make weekly trips home (for those country debriefings with God and family) a regular part of my life. Yes, I spent lots of time on Interstate 65 rolling between Biloxi, Mississippi and Century, Florida— thank God for traveling mercies each time I went.

As time went on, the weeks became months and I could hardly wrap my mind around the fact that it had been almost a year since that day when all that I had was taken away from me. One day, while studying the Word of God I found this life-producing scripture which prompted to call home and check on, "Chief," my mother; Ezekiel 18:28, "Because he considereth and turneth away himself from all his iniquities which he hath wrought, he shall surely live, and not die." I soon discovered that Chief had been hiding a very serious illness from me. Like most mothers, they always want to protect their children from bad news, which is pretty understandable considering my flood of negative news. She finally gave in to my prying and pushing and let me know that she was being treated for cancer. Remembering the Word I read in Ezekiel 18:28, I felt compelled to reassure her that the illness she faced was not unto death.

You may be wondering why I call my mother Chief. You see, "Chief" is our family's term of endearment for her. She never took any backtalk from us or anyone else for that matter. Heck, being raised up under her made me ready for anything, including military boot camp.

After several slow months of chemotherapy, the time to remove the cancerous tumor was upon us. While I had been tied to my problems in Biloxi and absent during the chemotherapy, I really wanted to be there for the surgery and recovery. So I requested and was granted leave, allowing me to be there for my mom. It was more than a blessing to have a career that allowed me the flexibility I needed in that time. God had granted me the desires of my heart!

When I arrived at the medical center, I was told that the procedure had gone well and as planned. We all were thankful. Chief was released to go home after only a few days. I was ready and willing to do whatever it took to help with her recovery. It had been only five years earlier that I worked in the local hospital as a nurse's aide. I promise you, I never fathomed that I would one day assist my own mother with post-surgical recovery.

As the journey with her began, we decided to accept each day and consider it a blessing from God. We moved through this most difficult time by keeping her moving and flexing her muscles. Little by little things got better and glimmers of light started to show at the end of the tunnel. We looked at each new day as one without limits and filled with possibilities. Things were moving along just fine but I noticed that she was increasingly leaving more food on her plate after each meal. So my next step was to be more creative with the food in hopes of getting her to eat.

As I made my way to her bedroom, one morning to wake her for breakfast, I didn't realize that I'd be overcome with nostalgia. Standing in the entrance of her room, I paused for a moment, for the first time I looked around; I saw bits and pieces of her life's moments captured in an old picture. There she was standing with Mary, one of my older sisters, and her husband Nathan, all smiling on what looked like a sunny day. Tucked in the edge of another picture frame were several small school-day photographs. There was one of Trent and Tess, my younger brother and sister. On the wall at the foot of her bed was my great-grandmother's old 1926 Victrola, a hand cranked seventy-eight speed record player. This relic had stopped working years ago, but Chief thought it was a nice piece of furniture. I knew that it housed memories for her of my great-grandmother. It was one of the few things she had that reminded her of their loving relationship. Yes, everybody most certainly loved Mrs. Maggie Harris. Even after death, members of our family were still keeping ties to her. That old Victrola was a part of that. As I gazed upon the turntable, I saw the green material that had a grass-like resemblance and thought back to when my brother Trent and I used it for horseracing adventures. On top of it were flowers that grew up along the wall, which matched the silk ones that were placed around the room. On her dresser was an old wig stand, as children we would draw faces on the front of it for use in our make-believe theatrical productions. It was entertainment for our sister Tess who was born with Down syndrome.

Across from the dresser were her makeup and powder boxes. My brother and I would sneak into them and paint clown faces on each other when Chief was away at work. Then there were the old wine and glass bottles, remnants from Chief's younger days, which now were filled with food coloring and placed with care in the windowsills; these were her sunlight catchers of sort. Yes, it was as though I'd walked back in time, but the pressing matters of her care cut short my trip down memory lane. I thought this momentary diversion odd, seeing that I had passed through that door hundreds of times during those weeks and never gave thought to any of it. Somehow, in that moment, my heightened awareness made my surroundings vividly clear. Returning to the present, I said, "Good morning, Chief." Taking her hand that had been darkened from the chemotherapy, I asked, "How are you feeling and what would you like me to make for breakfast?" I realized I was nervously running on, so I paused to await her response. My mind still pinging, I thought to myself, If she does not start eating better she might have to return to the hospital. After awhile, she answered in her familiar, soft but mid-tone voice, "Just anything will do me." Looking at her, I felt sad and helpless. My knowledge of all the happenings in her life were limited to a few things at best, but from what I knew, she had experienced more than her share of real tough times, and this ugly illness was just one more battle she had to fight. Regardless of one's faith, the question, "Why?" still comes to mind. Why did she have to endure something like this? I did not have an answer but I was glad to be there with her. I felt honored to be her son and to have her as my mother. I could still see a mother's love for her son. It was her selflessness. In spite of all her troubles, it was obvious that she was still mourning over the recent woeful events of my life. Even though at times she ran her household like a drill sergeant, when we needed her to be momma she was there.

Just about the time I became old enough to read, I was given a Bible by my second grade teacher's husband. As a child, I read in this book that I should honor my parents.

Well, the honor we had for Chief wasn't because of a law. It had been earned through selfless love demonstrated time and time again. Her raising us while juggling multiple jobs without a car was love. We were not the easiest to train up, but somehow she managed to get us through childhood, adolescent stages and into adulthood. She had been the one constant in our lives. It didn't matter that things weren't always good; instead we knew that at the end of the day she would be there. It was those fond memories that made me want her to know that everything would be all right.

I can remember the first time I realized that my mother, our Chief, was vulnerable. It was one afternoon I had just returned home from school. I had walked home from the bus stop curiously alone that day. When I entered the house something didn't feel quite right. The house was not opened up at all. The window that was usually ajar was closed and mama's curtains that were normally open were still drawn. This really caught my attention because I knew she would be up and about by that time. I dropped everything I was carrying and hurried to her room calling her all the while. I could hear a soft whimper in response to my calls. I struggled to locate where it was coming from. As I pulled back the curtains I found my mother (who in our eyes was super-mom,) in a fetal position on the floor. She seemed to be in pain and unable to take her pajamas off. She had been stuck that way all day and unable to call anyone or get to the door to signal for help. It was hard for me to believe, that she had been alone that entire day. As I began to assist her, it was then that I knew she more than needed our help. The strong woman who had worked tirelessly at three to four jobs weekly, just to keep food on the table and a roof over our heads was in desperate need. This revelation had taken place no more than ten years earlier.

So help is why I was presently there and help is what I intended to do. Now, the matter of making the meal was a different story. I could cook of course, but I felt like I needed help, so I prayed for God to help me. I had experienced poor success getting her to eat the evening before, and I did not want to fail again. With that in mind I began to pull out all the stops. I made biscuits, grits, country-pork sausage and sliced some fresh fruit. With all of this cooking going on, I knew the aroma would make its way back into her bedroom. In response to her aromatic visitor, she called out, "Child, that really smells good! As a matter of fact, I'm feeling a little hungry." "Thank you Jesus," I whispered. "Finally, she might start eating again."

After a little coaxing, we walked very carefully to the table. The whole while, I was prayerful that somehow her appetite would not be fleeting as it had been. As she got to the table, she started to go on and on about the breakfast spread, "Boy, just look at the food, you really didn't have to do all this. It all looks so good." I responded, "Now all you need to do is take a seat and eat." Still feeling the soreness from the surgery, she carefully eased her body into the chair. We paused for a moment to ask the blessing over the food, and then she began to eat. I could see that she was pleased, if for nothing else because of the effort that went into making the meal. Even if she was being kind to satisfy me, at least she was eating. I was overjoyed! As we began conversing and eating I realized I might have been wrong about her only eating to appease me. I noticed during our conversation the slight bobbing of her head, a sure sign that she was genuinely enjoying herself. Although it was only 132 miles away from Keesler Air Force Base (AFB), which was my assigned base at the time, I felt a world away from all of my troubles. It's amazing what a year of living a joyful life had done for me. I had learned to appreciate every moment that I was blessed to experience. This moment was precious.

As we sat eating, Chief nonchalantly, in her high pitched voice and southern twang said, "Boy, I wonder, whatever happened to Jacqui? I really believed she was your wife." Whew! That statement really caught me by surprise! At the time I wasn't looking for anybody's wife let alone a wife for myself. I quickly dismissed the whole question remembering the recent terrors I had gone through. Please understand that it wasn't as though Jacqui wasn't a nice woman, in fact in my eyes she was wonderful. However, understanding my unfinished-history with Carol, Jacqui had chosen to be out my life, and I had accepted her decision and moved on. That relationship had sailed downstream and I was not on the boat with it.

I guess I should take a moment to explain a bit further about Jacqui. She was a lovely young lady I had met a few years earlier, in 1987, after Carol left me the first time — prior to DJ's birth. Even though we shared the same faith, Jacqui and I thought it best to end our brief but loving relationship. In a nutshell, we met and we fell in love during the time I was in the process of petitioning for a divorce. It was during the time when Carol, had chosen to walk out of my life while pregnant with DJ. At that point in our marriage, it was so dicey that I wasn't really sure if it was my child. When the complications of my life became apparent to Jacqui she decided for Christ's sake it would be best to have nothing else to do with me. My marriage was broken long before Jacqui and I met and she quickly became an important part of my life. Even though I had legal and biblical cause to file for divorce, Jacqui did not want to give place for anyone to say she had played a role in breaking up my marriage. Walking away was a tough decision for her to make because she cared for me, but I completely understood and respected her choice. I can remember her quoting the Bible, "Let not your good be evil spoken of." Her decision eventually led to her writing a "Dear John" letter addressed to yours truly. It was a very brief and concrete goodbye. I guess it was the best thing for the both of us. Neither of us attempted to reach the other or rekindle the flame we once had. I knew and accepted that that relationship was over. I accepted that we had both moved on with our lives. I told Chief that I wasn't looking for anyone and that I was all right, and we continued enjoying our normal morning conversation. However, the human mind doesn't always function with logic. It has its own modality. Have you ever noticed at the mention of a single name, or with a waft of familiar cologne, our memories can come flooding back? Or perhaps when someone says something and it triggers a torrent of memories? Let me just say that by the end of that day at my mom's house, all I could think about was Jacqui. I wondered where she might be and if she had any thoughts left of me. My thoughts of her were overwhelming and the ghost of not knowing her status haunted me. It had gotten to the point that I found myself unwittingly hooked on the thought that there was still a chance for Jacqui and I to be together. Yes, it is really a remarkable thing the way the mind works; you can work diligently to try to forget an event of great significance and think that you've been successful. However, it only takes one word, a slight nudging, then distant memories can seem as though they occurred only yesterday. The simple words spoken by my mother were the bait that turned my heart towards the path that only

God knew the end of. Pressed by this feeling, I took it upon myself to try and reach her. The quickest way to reach her at the time was by phone. We didn't have internet service, people finders, or search engines then. So I anticipated it would take much effort to locate her. As I began to think of where to start, I remembered she was planning to move to Boston with her mother after she graduated from college. So, I deduced that it was as simple as calling and asking for a listing of all the Jacqui Thompsons in the Boston area. I had to tread through multiple operators and repeat myself constantly before an operator would give me a listing. When I finally received the listings, the grand total was seven for the name I was looking for. After looking them over, I began to promptly dial the numbers for each listing. I felt my heart palpitating in anticipation with every ring. Now, I was not aware of the male to female ratio in the Boston area. As I called the numbers and introduced myself, I came to realize these ladies were running short on qualified suitors. During one of my calls, one young lady said she would be my Jacqui. After calling and leaving messages over and over, my hope began to fade. Before it was all said and done I had spoken with several males who weren't at all pleased about me calling their woman. Nonetheless, I trudged on until every name on the listing had been called and heard from. Soon fear started to set in. So what's a guy to do? I soon realized the answer was to pray! Abandoning the phone, I went into the back hallway and got down on my face and cried out to the Lord and said, "Lord if Jacqui is supposed to be my wife have her call me. It is Christmas Eve and I have worked hard at my little efforts, so I place the whole matter in your hands." In this small prayer I released the situation into God's hands and knew somehow, someway he would work it all out. The events leading up to that moment caused me to think back on the entire affair. Where we met, how we grew to love each other, our adventures at church, and our visit to my hometown. Every memory I had of us being together was pleasant and enjoyable. My mind filled with thoughts as I thought about the events in my life at that time with Jacqui, the events which eventually led to her decision and our parting ways.

Chapter 3:
The Unexpected Hook Up

In January 1987 I was living in the military dorms due to my financial and marriage situation (my divorce from my pregnant wife, Carol, was not yet official). This was the third time she had chosen to leave me. While things looked bleak, I was actually experiencing a season of favor, a testimony to what is written: promotion comes from the Lord and the Lord sets one up and another down. I was living in the dorms because of that favor. It was because of my commander's special effort, and my favor with him, that I had a room. The standing policy was the unaccompanied permanent-party dorms were for Air Force members whose spouses were not in the area or at the base with them. In my case, my spouse was in the area, but we were separated. My situation was not one that granted residency in the dorms.

I remember the cold wintry evening that January when I first laid eyes on Jacqui—she was breathtaking. I was on my way to wash up for dinner and was taken by the presence of this young woman whose face almost seemed to shine. It was obvious that she was a new face. What struck me was that not only was she a new face, but also she was a bright face. She wasn't dressed in the typical "single and available" attire at all, just simple athletic wear. She looked so radiant and refreshing I couldn't help pausing to gaze at her from across the way. Hoping she would not feel my eyes as I tried to understand what was so different about her presence. In my mind an internal battle had already begun. I could not stop myself from asking, Why would she want to know me? What do I have to offer? I didn't realize it, but I had begun walking toward her. It was as if something or someone was leading me. Suddenly, there I was standing squarely in front of her. Not wanting her to feel accosted, I stepped back and gave her the brightest smile I could muster. She returned the smile and a conversation ensued.

It started with me asking, in my best stereophonic voice, "May I help you find something?" She replied with the most wonderful soothing voice, "I'm looking for a place to eat." I wasn't sure why, but something made me want to know this young lady. I had never met a woman quite like this one and I wasn't going to just let her go without discovering more about her. Even though I knew I was taking a risk, I hoped for the good that might happen. Her answer to my question was a perfect opportunity to extend a kind invitation so I replied, "There is a cafeteria in this dorm but you really don't want to eat here. You should consider eating elsewhere. I will gladly take you somewhere nice to eat." Without wincing or batting an eye after my invite, I waited for her response. I figured her answer would be slow, maybe even a decline. I had no idea it would require a forty-five minute biblical examination and life-history speech. It began with her asking me if I was saved and what salvation meant to me. She then wanted me to explain in detail my childhood salvation story, which happened to occur at the age of six. I quickly recalled that precious moment in my life when I accepted Christ in my heart through Billy Graham's radio crusade. I had to further explain who my pastor was, where I attended church and every Sunday school lesson for past three months! I would have never guessed that a simple question could turn into such an in-depth conversation. After I presented my life and salvation story she finally consented to a fifteen-minute road snack.

I would like to take a moment to let all the men out there know that if you are going to present yourself to a woman of excellence, you better be ready to back up what you offer. I promise you no woman of real substance wants a fake man. Ladies, you should already have your standards set, instead of trying to figure out how to behave according to a man. Your standards should be based on your faith and God's ability to meet all your needs according to his riches in glory!

This was certainly one of the most intriguing and challenging conversations I had had in a while. I had to find a way to make my approved fifteen minutes count. This was quite a change for me, I normally spent my evenings with a Christian family that adopted me, fed me, and kept me accountable for Christian living. As a single man in Mississippi, I needed a peaceful place for those nights when I was feeling tempted and tired.

So how was I going to make the most of this opportunity? I decided on a restaurant that would offer a quick sandwich, but would take about an hour to commute allowing us plenty of time to talk. As we drove along the road to Gulfport, Mississippi, I began to pursue her. I inquired about her childhood experiences, and she shared several of her adventures and experiences growing up in Boston.

Jacqui definitely had standards and set goals for what she wanted out of life. In fact she was only in Biloxi as a result of one of her prayers to God. About two years earlier Jacqui had joined the Air Force reserves because the pressure of working two and three jobs to pay for college became too much for her. On our extended drive to dinner she recounted how she happened to join the reserves: She had driven a friend to take the Armed Services Vocational Aptitude Battery (ASVAB) test and decided that she would also take it since she had nothing else to do. After the test a recruiter called her and asked if she would like to join the Air Force reserves. Although she was leary, she felt impressed to give it a try. She chuckled as she retold the conversation she and her father had after the recruiting visit; the recruiter said she would have to lose twenty pounds in the next three weeks. She told her father that if it was the Lord's will for her to join He would remove the weight because she was too busy to focus on weight loss. He then took her to McDonald's for lunch. Three weeks later she showed up for the follow-up test fairly certain that she would not pass, as she had not tried to loose any weight, only to be informed that she had lost twenty-five pounds. She was stunned. She felt perhaps God was providing another path for college tuition, so she joined. She felt that boot camp and basic training were primarily for her spiritual growth and she used her time there for study and reflection. She went on to tell me that although she enjoyed the training she absolutely hated wearing steel-toe boots because they hurt her ankles. She was in training to be a loadmaster and she had to wear boots. One day she was at lunch during a weekend drill and ran into an older gentleman who was a Chaplain's Assistant. They sat and talked for about 30 minutes. She told the gentleman that she would love to work in his field. About six months later while she was in training on driving vehicles, she was called in and informed she had a gentleman visitor. As she entered the hanger, some of the guys joked with her about her 'visitor friend.' She did not recognize him until he recounted their conversation. He said to her, "I have a slot for you to become a Chapel Assistant if you want it. You have to attend a six-week training January. I have done all of the paper work requesting your transfer, so you are set to go." It was November 1986. Jacqui was to complete college in December. At first, she was hesitant because her father had passed away just one year earlier around the same time and she did not want to leave her mother alone. The gentleman reminded her of her father though. He was a tall, thick fellow, shortened by the arching of his shoulders. He had a half-moon hairline and soft smile. She recounted that she was amazed about all he had done without her even asking. This was the first time she had seen him since the conversation in the chow hall six months earlier. She took his sudden appearance as an answer to prayer for her to be delivered from those steal-toe boots. She resolved to say yes. Now, there she was, sitting beside me. I too shared many of my childhood stories, though she would occasionally say that she didn't believe some of them.

Chapter 4:
A Refreshing Change

It was truly heaven on earth as we rode together sharing and laughing. As we ate and talked, it became evident that she was uncomfortable with my height. She was possibly one inch shorter than me and tried to adjust her austere posture by rounding her shoulders a bit and bending her knees. I, on the other hand, felt like I had a beautiful amazon woman who should not be ashamed of her stature and I told her so. Thankfully, she became more interested in the quality of our conversation than the visual presentation of our stance.

She was one of the nicest girls I had ever met. I decided to pursue her with everything that I could remember about winning the heart of a woman. Granted, I really didn't have any money or any real promise of a good life, just hope and faith in God. I can remember the efforts I made to woo her. We had our places to eat and hang out, but we also had the special places as well. I remember our first special date. I took her to Chin's Garden. It was an enjoyable evening although she had no idea that I borrowed money from my pastor to take her out. I mean, what I can say—a guy's got to do what a guy's got to do. I can recall the carefully worded explanation I gave to my pastor as I asked him to help me. He and I were standing in the fellowship hall discussing his schedule for the next week, when he asked about my availability. I was a bit nervous because not only was I about to tell my pastor that I may not be available, but I also needed him to loan or, preferably, give me some money to take out my special date. So standing there, shaking in my shoes, I just blurted it out, "Pastor, I will not be available, because I need you to loan or give me some money to take my friend to eat at a special restaurant!" There was a moment of deafening silence, followed by whole barrage of questions, "Brother DeWayne, is this the young lady from Sunday service and Bible study? Where is she from? How did the two of you meet?" These questions were followed by others, which were intended to safeguard me from entering a relationship similar to the marriage I was in the process of getting out of. I suppose I answered well because at the end he gave me the money and I was off to arrange the particulars posthaste.

It turned out to be a great evening and everything went as planned. She seemed pleased at my effort to demonstrate her importance to me. In the course of chatting I soon discovered that this lovely young lady was a real junk-food junkie. A good hamburger, fries, and a shake were heaven for her. In addition to her love for fast food, she made me aware of her love for pizza. She liked simplicity in life and it was the simple things that I enjoyed most about her. Even more, I enjoyed the hours we would spend just sharing our thoughts and insight on inspired revelation of God's word. One of the areas that we would often discuss was the Gifts of the Spirit. Believe me, we would get into some real heated debates regarding this area, especially the matter of speaking in unknown tongues. I can remember us going back and forth often on this subject. My Christian experience was that of a more conservative and less charismatic nature. Now don't get me wrong, I had seen this manifestation, but I believed it was given to some people and that it was not available to everyone. While from her experience it was the only way you could truly experience the fullness of

God. I recall her quoting the Bible, "You really shouldn't answer before you have heard the whole matter." This was the usual for us as we tooled along in her orange-tinged, white Ford Mustang that had been stained by the red Dixie clay of Alabama. At the end of our debates and conversations, we would always agree that we didn't know everything, and that both of us had more to learn.

As we learned more about each other, time moved too swiftly and the reality of the brief time we would have together became a haunting realization. Jacqui was into her third week of training for her reserve duty. I knew that if we were going get to know each other, we would have to do it quickly or the possibilities of falling in love—well, it just wasn't going to happen. The thoughts of our journey and how we fell in love brings to mind our first kiss. It was February, the sun was about to set, and we were parked by the flight line at the edge of Back Bay. There was a chill in the air and the sky was painted with beautiful hues of crimson and fuchsia. The radio played, "I will be yours till the end of time, until time stands still..." softly in the background as we sat together. When the moment was right, I kissed her and she kissed me. It was apparent from her smile and blushing-eyes of approval that she was falling for me. There we were, embraced, as the sun set. What an incredible moment! I was definitely in love.

It was the day before Valentine's Day and I decided to express my love for her in the classiest way I could afford. I bought her a dozen red long-stem roses and a bottle of the perfume I had observed her enjoying while we were out window-shopping a few days earlier. On this evening, I had been invited to present a rendition of a Dr. Martin Luther

King Jr. speech. I thought dropping off her present on my way to the event would be perfect. I had hoped that she would be impressed with the gift and the giver. When I presented my tokens to her, she loved them both. And the maneuver of the visit paid off. She was very complimentary of my attire that evening. I was sporting my grandfather's Cleveland Butler specials; for everyone else, it was my black suit, accompanied by my narrow black Armani tie and burgundy wing tips shoes. I was feeling really good and thought I looked good too. I know you must be thinking, He must really think he's something right now. Well, just let me say, I was walking like one of those fellows in the Ebony Fashion Fare. I tell you, I wanted the world to know that I had a wonderful girl, and she was all mine. She really did put music in my heart and gave my step a new bounce. Jacqui was resisting her emotions to fully embrace her developing feelings; I however, was on cloud nine. Judging by the look in her eyes, I was winning whatever battle she may have been fighting. She continued to put up a good verbal fight and insisted on reminding me that the relationship would never work. I heard her sincerely-stated words. I had to decide if I was going to continue to pursue her or let it be. I thought for a brief moment, and chose to continue my pursuit.

Chapter 5:
The Family Hook Up

I was in love and I wanted the whole world to know about it, but most of all, I wanted to introduce the woman of my dreams to my mother. My main motivation was to persuade Jacqui that this relationship could work. My last relationship did not start in a very appropriate fashion and I wanted to do things the right way this time. Before I moved any further, I wanted and needed my mother's approval. So, I decided to let Jacqui know what I wanted to do. The next day, I went by her room with the intent to ask her out for dinner. As I approached her dorm room, I ran the potential scenario back and forth through my mind. On our way to dinner that night, I mulled over my carefully-worded proposition. It wasn't until after dinner that I made up my mind and knew exactly what I was going to say. There is something about a satisfied pallet that can affect one's confidence. We had both finished our meals, so it was just as good a time as any. Throwing my carefully crafted plan out the door, I just leaned back in my chair and asked her to come home with me and meet my family. Her response was hesitant, "I really don't have anything to wear to meet your mother." I replied, "Well then, let's go get something." After a little persuasion, she finally relented and we went shopping for a few things.

She purchased a long, pale denim cowgirl skirt with white lace on the bottom, a beautiful white shirt and white sagging cowboy boots. As we strolled along passed the jewelry shops I notice her face light up when I pointed out a small, opal ring. The attendant at the jewelry shop had also noticed and asked me why I thought it was so beautiful. "It's not harsh like other stones but it is soft and filled with a warm yet brilliant glow, kind of like her," I explained with an affectionate look towards Jacqui. I secretly purchased the opal ring as a little something extra to share with her the next day. I only wanted to say thank you to her for agreeing to come with me to meet my family. The next day I presented Jacqui with the special gift I had purchased, an opal pendant and ring set which she loved and treasured. I was pleased and very excited about our upcoming journey. It was quite the opposite with Jacqui. She was filled with trepidation and anxiety. As she listened to the excitement in my voice, she could tell that I believed all would be well and that my mother would be glad to finally meet her. In her mind, she just knew that I was wrong and that my mother would quietly pull her aside and whisper in her ear, "Sweet girl, I'm sure you mean well, but DeWayne is a married man." And with that short comment she would be politely shown the door. In fact, Jacqui was hoping that her predictions would actualize, providing the scenario that would once and for all end this escapade.

The night we arrived, she was received with the warmest of welcomes. My mother, Mrs. Evelyn "Chief" Thomas, was the epitome of good old southern hospitality, a combination of gentleness and warmth. She quickly laid aside the formalities and didn't waste any time letting Jacqui know how pleased she was that I had found a nice girl. She openly admonished me to treat Jacqui right or I would have to deal with the Chief herself. Jacqui almost fell off of her chair, she was counting on being turned around at the door and sent back to Mississippi. The night was a typical evening at home, full of conversation and recounting of childhood stories. It was an evening full of laughter and fun, which came to a close all too quickly. When it came time to bed everyone down, to Jacqui's surprise, Chief insisted on giving up her room. Jacqui would have gladly slept in the extra bed in my little sister's room, but after a little convincing; she decided to go along with the family tradition.

To her surprise, she had one of the most comfortable nights of sleep in a long while. In fact she was still resting, when all of a sudden, she was awakened by my booming voice followed rapid knocking at the door. I suppose I can be a bit heavy-handed when I'm nervous, but I had orders from Chief to get Jacqui up, so Aunt Mary Lee could meet her. I wondered to myself how Jacqui would take to this early morning interlude with my family. Standing in the doorway, I told Jacqui that Aunt Mary Lee wanted to meet her and was waiting outside. She hurriedly raced to the bathroom to prepare for the early morning introductions. While she was in the bathroom, I began to hear voices that sounded like people gathering outside. I wasn't sure what happened between the time she started dressing and the time she finished, but it was certainly too late to figure it out. Before we could ask any questions, we heard my mother calling people, inviting what were apparently other family members, excitedly, "Come on in and meet DeWayne's new girl friend." This was not my plan at all; my plan was to keep the morning simple. Jacqui, my mother, and a few select family members were the only people on my introduction list for the morning. At this point all I could do was try and maintain my composure, as I watched my plan quickly slip out of my control. There it was, true to form, a hilltop hospitality reception. I found myself thinking, Jacqui is going to think we are all crazy.

I followed cautiously behind Jacqui as she walked through the living room, and looked into the kitchen. At first glance she and I noticed the back door was slightly ajar, but after mmlooking carefully we could see and hear ten or fifteen people waiting in line to meet and greet her. They were dressed in what appeared to be special outfits as if it were a holiday. Jacqui later revealed she was thinking, These people must have lost their minds, don't they know I'm the other woman? But they weren't thinking that at all. They had been hoping for a better life and good wife for me, their native son, and whether she knew it or not she fit the bill perfectly. She soon came to realize just how much suffering they had witnessed me go through, and how much joy and hope they believed she would bring into my life. It was amazing.

I watched Jacqui, a very quiet and reserved person, become a very gregarious hostess. She put on her best face and greeted them with the same enthusiasm she received. She met many friends of the family and people from the community center. Soon she learned that my mother had several other nick names—"Rabbit," "The Baby," and of course "Chief." Jacqui chose to use Chief. When I asked her about it, she said, "I thought I should use Chief since it seemed more than acceptable among the younger members of the family." My sisters Dorothy "Dot," Mary Jo, Alfreda and Tess, and a host of other family members were so encouraging. They all had something good to say about Jacqui. Jacqui was amazed as she heard them speak so well of her. She couldn't help but think that they were speaking of someone else, especially since they had only recently met. Later that morning, Mrs. Creola Fountain, the queen of chat and oration, came by. Everyone seemed to have a story to tell or was a part of a story. Jacqui felt very much at home and felt that she could come to enjoy all of it.

Seeing that Jacqui was settling in and the day was moving fast, I began to prepare and set up one of the most important barbeques of my life. I had mentioned to Jacqui that I was going to cook some ribs. Not just any ribs, but these would be the ribs that would help me win her over. Of course I didn't mention any of that to her, but I did wonder why she hadn't gotten excited about my announcement to barbeque. My curiosity led me to then ask what kind of sauce she liked. Her response was, "I'm not sure. I really don't care very much for ribs." She added, "I would prefer a good grilled burger any day over ribs." I thought to myself, I've got my work cut out for me. But before I could do anything I needed to take a quick trip up to the local grocery store. It seemed everybody and their mother was at the store. At every turn somebody was walking up to us asking how I was doing and inquiring about Jacqui for an introduction. It took us almost an hour to just pick up a few things. After returning home I worked my skills until the end of the day adjusting and modifying the meat and sauce until I thought they were perfect. After which I presented them on a platter along with some bake beans, coleslaw, corn on the cob and some hot rolls. It was the first time I had made ribs for the folks back home. It started with my sister, Alfreda, conducting her taste test. Her response was "Tang, these ribs are good." (Tang is an old childhood nickname of mine, short for Tangle-foot.) Then Chief gave me a good review, "Boy, these ribs are really good." Finally the person of my inspiration had tasted them. She ate all that was on her plate and returned for more. That was it! She had fallen in love with my cooking and I knew everything was going to work out. Yes sir, all was well in my new, safe little world. There I was in what seemed to be the perfect world and by comparison it was. I guess to top it all off Jacqui, who really did not like ribs, had fallen in love with me, my barbecue, my family, and town. I was so thankful that words could not express my gratefulness in that moment. The day was coming to an end and it was about time for Jacqui and me to start making our way back to Biloxi and the real world.

On our way back her disappointment regarding her desired outcome of our visit grew more obvious as our drive brought us closer to Biloxi. It was apparent to me that she was more determined to move further away from me. I could feel it in my heart. I could sense the cords that bound us together loosen and weaken as the thoughts of separation were being infused by Jacqui's determination to do what was she felt was right in the eyes of the Lord. I knew she was correct about the timing, but I believed I was justified and God's grace would cover it all. Throughout the ride I asked her if all was well and she would reply with a simple, "Everything is fine." In my little mind I still had a chance. But the truth is, the Holy Spirit had made His move also and began to guide her to become even more resolute about her internal decision to cut off our burgeoning relationship. I thought I had sealed the deal with the barbecue ribs and my wonderful family. It looked as if my secret recipe was not enough. I was in for a real battle.

Chapter 6:
A Hold on the Hookup

As we arrived at her dorm room I gave her a hug and kissed her and expressed again how I felt about her and how wonderful my family believed she was. As always she smiled, but this time she was almost in tears. Now, I want you to know something about me. It only takes a little bit to start my fountain of tears to flowing. So when she started, I started. I so wanted her to be happy, but it was evident that this was not the case. I wondered if I had somehow offended her back at the house. Or perhaps maybe one of my friends may have said something inappropriate to her. Deep down inside I knew I was only fooling myself. I could see the resolve in her eyes but I continued in the role, hoping that I might somehow stumble upon something solid to use in support of my case for the relationship. It may have been a shot in the dark to ask, but I had to know what was going on. Looking into her eyes I asked, "Can you please share with me what's on your heart?" Taking my hand and sitting down on the steps she began to share, "DeWayne, regardless of how you look at this matter, the fact is you are still married. And even if you are separated right know I'm not sure about this entire situation. I really have to spend some time praying about this. I feel God speaking to me and I have to let you know this was not the way our falling in love was supposed to happen." What an incredible shock to my heart. In that moment all I could think was, Oh my God! If I don't do something fast I'm going to lose her right now. So trying to be the wise and sensible one, I suggested that we shouldn't make any final decisions, "You will be returning to Birmingham this week end and I'm scheduled to go on a TDY (Temporary Duty Assignment). Why don't we let this rest awhile and when we have given it some thought, perhaps we can better decide?" With that being said, I thought it best to make a quick exit so she wouldn't have time to say anything else.

The next day or so was difficult to say the least. I was pulling out every stop that I could think of to convince Jacqui not to end the relationship and give us a chance. At the same time she was not pulling any punches. She was determined to bring the whole thing to a quick end. Knowing her opinion on the matter, I did the only thing that came to my mind. I found an article in a magazine that said, the surest way to express your love when giving flowers is to give the person of your affection a single red rose. That was fortunate for me because I was getting very low on cash. I decided to get myself all dressed up, I even put on my best cologne, Pierre Cardin which is old school now, but at the time it was second to none.

As I made my way to her dorm room, anxiety was mounting. I could feel my palms become wet with perspiration. My knees were a bit shaky as I realized this was all I had left in my proclaimed love arsenal. This was one of the last "big guns" I had left. I knocked at her door and waited patiently for her to answer. I didn't realize as I stood there nervously waiting for her, she was on the phone talking with her best friend trying to rationalize the relationship. She opened the door and greeted me coolly. Her resolve to end this affair was evident. We sat in the lounge and talked for a while. She had not yet accepted the red rose I brought her. Instead she sat across from me and gave a weak reiteration of the rehearsed break up speech she had practiced with her friend on the phone. Her discourse was full of scriptural references accompanied with a plea for mercy from my relentless pursuit of her. She stated the stress of the internal conflict was more than she could bear. In fact she had missed her class that day because she was weary from sleeplessness and the tumultouse emotional battle that was raging within. She confessed that she cared more for me than she should. Her mind however, could not justify continuing in the relationship. She conceded that scripturally, I had every right to divorce my wife, however, the fact remained that I was separated, not divorced. Once again she echoed her mantra, "Let not your good be evil spoken of..." My mind however was focused on the fact that this was the woman of my dreams. I said softly, careful not to ruffle any feathers, "I understand." I took her hand and gently kissed the center of her palm and placed the long stem rose in it. She blushed as her resistance melted away. Whew! I thought, I'm still in the game. It was at this point I felt I had the victory. I thought to myself, I finally have her. I believe she is with me to stay! I thought a victory dinner would be in order so I asked her to accompany me to dinner at Pizza Hut.

As we rode to the restaurant it became apparent that perhaps my celebration was a bit premature. She was rebuilding her partitions faster than I could fathom. I was being torn away from her while still in her presence. I could feel myself loosing it. I pushed back the tears. I couldn't let her see me cry again. I couldn't go down like that! (I didn't want to violate the "man code." I couldn't cry twice in one week). I started to speak to myself silently saying over and over, Just settle down and think about something else. You can make it through this. Don't start crying right here in front of her. The tension was broken when I heard a familiar soft voice speaking as if all was well in the world, "What would you like thin or thick crust tonight?" To ease the pain of the experience, I went along with this ruse. We made small talk being careful to avoid any reference to the apparent ending of our relationship. We both wanted the night to last forever but the manager of the restaurant informed us that it was closing time. After driving awhile, we found ourselves on the beach talking about nothing in particular but holding on as if we were waiting for some kind of supernatural sign that it was all going to work out. I remember talking about my TDY to seven-level school and my follow-on orders to Yokota Japan. I said that it was going to be a real adventure. She shared her aspiration of one day owning a center for pregnant college students. Although the conversation was enjoyable, the day had to end. Jacqui had made plans to leave the following day. So we decided to try and get as much rest as possible with what little night that remained. I took her back to her room. As I escorted her to the door I took her into my arms and kissed her. In her eyes I saw that she was very vulnerable, but we made it through the night without falling into temptation. The next day, Sunday—the day of departure was finally upon us. I drove behind Jacqui to Mobile, Alabama finally letting her go as she made her way onto Interstate 65 North.

Chapter 7:
A Dear John Letter

As I made my way back to Biloxi, Mississippi I thought about the wonderful days I had spent with Jacqui. I was returning to my life, and still searching for even the slightest chance that the relationship could survive the onslaught of her spiritual intrepidness. If you have not noticed by now, I can be a bit tenacious. I was still hoping that somehow this thing would work out.

As the length of days between her calls became longer, my insatiable desire to hear from Jacqui grew stronger. Soon the calls from her became almost nonexistent. The time of departure for my TDY was upon me and I still hadn't heard a thing. I hoped that with me going away it would provide some distraction from the internal longing that clouded my world daily. When I would awake in the morning I could barely get out of bed knowing that she was all but gone out of my life. I think the stress of it all caused me to fall ill. The silence, the waiting, and the emptiness were almost too much to withstand. I wanted to pray but wasn't sure if it was right to pray that she not leave me. I think she almost convinced me that God would not bless our relationship, at least not in its current state. The key word in that statement is almost. I knew in my mind that letting go was right, but in my heart it was gut wrenching. I had boasted to any and everyone about this wonderful person named Jacqui. And of course there was the family, so when they would ask me about her, I would say things were going just fine, everything was perfect. Knowing inside it wasn't the truth, but what would they say if they knew the truth. They might think it was entirely my fault. I could already imagine what they would say, "You are the reason why no woman wants you." I was still holding out, but with time my stubborn pride died. I started to miss time with my Father and my God. I started to pray my way through and somehow things seemed to improve.

I reported to the base and began my six-week school for the coveted Dental Technician Seven Level. My supervisor and the dental Chief explained that the opportunity was made available to an elite few and was only open to those on a path for success. What a blessing! Somehow God had been watching out for me even though there were times when I knowingly did things to counter his plans for my life. The intensive pace of the school proved to provide a reprieve from the relentless thoughts of my memories with Jacqui. The homework assignments were like fingers reaching into every part of who we were. Our small class operated a simulated clinic, developing an annual budget with all of its trappings. We were required to conduct a mass casualty exercise, and also developed a process called "Work Group Dynamics." This forced us to work together for long hours, to see if we could maintain our boundaries and not become distracted.

I guess it was about midway through the course I was on my way to my dorm room, when I noticed a package placed at my door. Suddenly my heart pounded with anticipation of what it contained. Well, as you can imagine I ran to the door and before I could even get into the room I was ripping into the package, which to my surprise was somewhat heavy. As I opened the box, it became apparent that it was books. In addition to the books there lay a letter from Jacqui. I could hardly wait to read it. The letter started with a question, "Why do great men have to walk alone? Why must they climb mountains at least ten thousand feet tall?" The poem went on to a very absolute directive and truth—she, Jacqui, would not be the cause of death, nor could she be present during the death of a marriage. The words were crafted to inspire, to propel my faith towards Godly action. Instead they created a cascade of pain that riveted my soul leaving me listless. I paused and dropped heavily on my bed. I laid there in a blur of emotions. My mind flashed back to when I first started the school. I tried to dismiss the obvious fact that the relationship was over. I had known it before but the letter made me accept it now. I started to read on. She had one last request, for me to forget about her, to go on with my life, and return to the woman who had left me. She wanted me to read the books that were placed in the box. The reading material she sent was designed to help save marriages. I fell back on the bunk and pounded the bed with my fist. How could she do this? How could she just let me go and demand that I should go back to the women who had hurt me so badly? I sat there feeling numb and heartbroken. I couldn't eat anything; I just wanted to be alone. There wasn't anyone I wanted to talk to or anyone that I wanted to be around, so I drifted off to sleep.

The next morning I awoke and pushed the books under the bed and fell back into my school world. I thought I needed someone to distract me from all of the hurt and pain I was experiencing. It seemed the more I put myself out there, the more apparent it was that I was in no shape to enter into another relationship at that time. I had coworkers that were single and felt sorry for me, but in my mind I could only hear Jacqui's haunting words, "Go back to your wife and do everything you can to make your marriage work." Even though these words echoed in my mind I couldn't understand how Jacqui could have come up with this. I suppose that was just it, her thoughts were not of this world but rather Heavenly, of God. With that in mind, I thought maybe, just maybe, I should consider them.

I found myself literally compelled to reach under the bunk bed and pull out the books and begin reading. The first book was about restoring broken marriages. I don't remember the author's name but I can remember something about dating your mate. I was also given two other books that continue even today to be a part of my library. They are, If Satan Can't Steal Your Joy, he can't Touch Your Goods, by Jerry Sevelle; and The Blood Covenant, by Kenneth Copland. I slowly began to read them and they began to have a profound effect on my thought process. I was so intrigued after reading through the information, that I searched and found the biblical character that was mentioned in the book. After conducting my research about a man named Hosea and his wife Gomer, I discovered that there was no sin too big to forgive. The light it shed on forgiveness helped me to understand that it was ok to go and get my wife who left me. I wanted to be faithful to the Word but little did I know what fire I was about to enter into. Yes, a trial by fire. I would be tested and tempted in every aspect of my faith in God.

Chapter 8:
Unhitched...His Tale

The woman that I was in love with sent me a "Dear John" letter and advised me to reconnect to my wife. She must have thought I was nuts or something to think I would fall for that advice. I was on a very important TDY and the course load was not exactly easy. I was moving forward in my life. I went through a rough patch in my marriage, but somehow God had brought me out and I wasn't even close to thinking about getting back into the same situation. I decided to move on with my plans and leave for Japan. I was very excited and anticipated my completion of the Air Force's Dental Management School. I tried to stay focused on my plans but I kept hearing the words of the letter that Jacqui had written in mind saying, "You should try to work things out with your wife." I tried to think on other things, even attempted something new and went water skiing, although I didn't know how to swim. No matter how I tried avoiding Jacqui's words, they continued to invade my mind. So I talked to one of my classmates and she said I might need to seek closure in the matter. I wasn't sure, I only knew that something needed to happen.

What was I to do? How was I to go about doing this? Well, first I had to pray that I would be able to find out where Carol was staying. I called several numbers in Biloxi and asked around until I found her mother and was given a number for her sister Bonita. I was then able to reach her and expressed that I wanted to help her with the baby. At that time I wasn't sure if the child in her womb was mine. The emotions flowing through me were strange, as I had not felt a desire to reach out to her before that moment. It was as though some latent switch was turned on. I began to share with her why I was reaching out to her and how I was committed to making our marriage work. In response she invited me to come back to her place in Biloxi. The following weekend I decided to drive back to see her. It would only be one day but it was to demonstrate that I was genuine in what I said to her. Mind you, this was not a hop and a skip for me to reach her. It was more than 700 hundred miles one-way to Biloxi. I hoped she would see this gesture as a demonstration of my earnestness to make the marriage work— if only for the child's sake.

I drove through the night and around two o'clock Saturday morning I reached Biloxi. When I arrived at her home I felt a bit anxious but I went through with my plans anyway. I knocked at her door, she answered—and just like that I walked back into her world. While at her apartment we talked and shared some of the things that had taken place in our lives. As we talked, I listened hoping for some kind of sign that things could work out. I tried to believe what she said. I could sense her experiencing the same struggle. The mental play was almost too much to handle. I really wanted to trust her, but the desire to see for myself was there and I had to look. After all I was no fool and it had only been six months since the cause of our last separation.

During the first day of the visit she left without saying where she was going, only to return hours later with unexplained burn spots in her clothing. The next day I reluctantly waited for the chance to look through her belongings. That morning, when she announced that she needed to run out to get a few things for breakfast, I thought, now is my chance. As she left, I jumped up off the couch and quickly ran into her bedroom. I figured it would take her about twenty minutes or so to go to the grocery store. I purposed in my heart that if I found something I wasn't going to say anything, after all this was our first time together since the separation. I had quickly checked all of usual places. At first, I felt it was the right thing to do. I had somehow justified my invasion into her privacy. It was about ten minutes into my quick search that I was beginning to feel like maybe this was not such a good idea. Then I heard a key unlocking the door— she had returned earlier than expected! Now all I wanted to do was get out of her bedroom. I didn't want her to catch me conducting this impromptu search. Hastily I tried to put things back as they were, and just as the front door opened, I found a crack pipe. It had fallen out of a bundle of clothing as I rushed to put things back. I was devastated. There I was standing with the thing in my hand. What was I to do? I was busted. No, she was busted.

My plan of not confronting her was out the window. I attacked, demanding to know what the pipe was doing in her house. From there more questions followed, "Is this yours? How often are you using? How long have you been doing this?" By the time I ended my rant I realized I had pretty much crashed and burned. She calmly denied that it was hers and said it was someone else's. She said a friend had asked her to hold on to it for while. I could sense the disappointment in her voice. She didn't say it but I could tell that she was thinking, Here we go again. Then there were the tears welling up in her eyes. I wanted to believe her, but inside I feared my deepest concerns were becoming a reality. As we stood there, we experienced something that was totally new to us. There was an eerie silence as we made breakfast together. I thought silently, No screaming at me? She was completely non-retaliatory. A miracle had taken place and I began to think that maybe Jacqui was right. After that I was even more determined to help her and the unborn child. Things seemed to be going smoothly, so I thought it was a good idea to bring up how we could work things out. We managed to get through a few topics while other areas were too sensitive to even communicate. The conversation started to loop and I realized I should slow down and ease into it. In an attempt to keep things civil, I quickly changed the topic. Knowing that the subject of her father had always been a positive one, I inquired about how he was doing. I had to think realistically; Rome was not built in a day so it was best to take it slow. Before long my time spent with her was over and I was on the road again to Texas.

The return trip seemed much shorter than the trip there. In record time I made it back to Sheppard AFB, Wichita Falls, Texas. Yes, Texas had been good to me and all I needed to do now was complete my course. It was only a few short weeks in time before what had started out to be a long escape had come to a quick end. With the intensity of the course winding down, I spent my last few weeks pondering what I could do to mark this fresh start in my life. One day I drove by a car dealership and made a flash decision to trade in my VW Rabbit, but I had a difficult time letting her go. You see, she was my first brand new car and I loved her more than I had realized. However, after graduating, I found myself at the Toyota dealer just outside of town. There, I purchased a minivan—a true testament to my decision to be a family man.

As Carol and I continued to talk we decided to work things out and move into the military base housing. It was a practical decision since we were expecting a new baby and would need to save as much money as possible. Once we moved into base housing, we tried to become a happy family, or so I thought. Even with the new commitment budding and the promise of a child in our future, things were taking an interesting turn. I noticed that with each passing day the romance and excitement of the renewed relationship was diminishing. Each day I would return home I would find Carol with a new set of old friends.

I can recall one evening she went out and stayed very late. By the time she returned it was well after midnight. To say the least I was a bit concerned but so tired of her excuses I didn't bother asking where or with who she had been. I simply asked her not to stay out late without letting me know where she was. Her reply was, "You know I'm just with my friends talking." I pleaded with her and said, "For the baby's sake please try to get proper rest." I still had my suspicions. On several occasions I noticed marijuana-seed burns in clothes. I wanted to bury my questions in a grave of indifference, but the words just flew out of my mouth all at once, "Carol please, please stop smoking that stuff, if not for you, then for the baby." She denied it again. I ask her again to please stop with the drugs; I let her know that the baby's life was important to me. Unfortunately, the very next night she stayed out late again only this time until four in the morning. After sitting up worrying, I became angry. I wanted her to know just how furious I was. I thought, I will lock her out. That will teach her a lesson on pregnant-wife etiquette. So I got out of bed and made my way to the living room and the front entrance. Not thinking about how Carol would react, I put the dead bolt on the door and decided to return to bed. As I was on my way upstairs to bed, I contemplated if I should have told her twin nieces, who were living with us, not to touch the door and to come get me if Carol came home. Just as I was about to lie down there was a knock at the door. It was Carol and she was demanding that I open the door right then. Her voice was much louder than necessary and I'm sure she was disturbing the neighbors at that point. I asked her to stop yelling first and then I would let her in. Putting the chain on first, I cracked the door to ask her where she had been. By this time the twins had come out of their rooms and I glanced over to them and saw they were becoming afraid. At that moment Carol lost it and began to beat on the glass with her bare hand. Then it happened. The glass broke resulting in a serious cut on her left hand. A few minutes later the police arrived, our neighbors had called them. As it turns out I happened to know the police sergeant who came by, which was the only reason he didn't arrest one of us. Instead he asked the two of us what was going on. After I explained, he called the ambulance to take us to the hospital. I already knew that as a base resident the situation was bound to get back to my superiors at work.

Sure enough, the next day I was in the commander's office. I was very afraid and with much trembling in my prayer unto God I stood before the commander explaining what happened and how it was all an accident. Though I had worked closely with commander and had a great relationship with him, our relationship was in jeopardy. I knew if this kind of thing continued to occur without being resolved it would become a problem for me at my work place.

As I thought back on the how the entire affair between Carol and I began, I was convicted because it was I who had crossed the line that night in the nightclub. It was several years earlier, in the fall of 1984, when we first met. She explained that she was separated from her husband and that she had children. At that time I justified my actions telling myself that if it was o.k. with her, it was o.k. with me. My experience taught me that I was at fault, because instead of keeping my distance, upon meeting her I did not regard her as a wife with a husband and family. I was the one who opened the proverbial Pandora's Box. When I came to myself that very same night, I let her know that I couldn't see her again. This was my very best attempt at making things right. I remember thinking, What else can I do to halt this thing before it goes too far? I decided that I should leave town to let things cool down for a while. I was in way over my head and I thought I could confide in my partner in crime Roy Holt. Unfortunately, I had forgotten his personal mantra "If you did not share the same womb with her then she is fair game. This meaning it was o.k. to sleep with her." So he really did not see any harm in my little one-time interlude. I told him that I was going home to Century to let things cool down a bit and I would be back the next week.

At home I was enjoying the typical lively conversation with my family when I noticed that one of my nieces was at the door. She stood there and announced that someone named Carol was outside and wanted to see me. My heart sank. Arising from my chair to peer out of the window to confirm what had been said, I saw her standing there with folded arms. It was then that I realized my friend, Roy, had given her directions and that was how the whole thing started. At the time I thought it would be all right. She needed help out of a bad situation and I was there. I was under constant conviction about our relationship and tried to make a wrong thing right by getting married. The truth about my contributions to the situation compelled me to be more than willing to try to make things better and help her through this difficult time. Now, it was apparent that I really had no idea of the implication of my actions.

Chapter 9:
A Higher Call: Can this Child Live?

With much prayer we waded through the quagmire of the next few months as we hoped that the birth of our child might somehow bring new life to the faltering effort. Our relationship was tenuous at best. The sweltering heat of summer was taxing even the best air conditioners. Everything came to a climax August 1987. As usual, I was exhausted and my stress level was at an all-time high; it seemed as if it was tangible, I could feel it when I entered a room. The tension started a few days earlier when I had come home for lunch and Carol wasn't there. Normally it wouldn't be an issue, but the doctor had warned us that she was two weeks overdue and her water could break at any time. Knowing this, I anxiously called around but could not locate her. I hoped for the best but it was one of those times when my fear and a little anger had overtaken me. If I had any sense of professionalism it would be my duty to try and isolate my personal life from work. With that in mind, I decided to press on about my day.

When I got home that evening I found her there and hoped to keep my questions and concerns over the matter to myself. Unfortunately the memories and the image of the crack pipe that I found a few months earlier were seared in my mind. I had to know. So I just blurted it out, "Where were you this afternoon? I called around and couldn't find you. Have you been... well... doing that stuff?" She responded, "What stuff?" I said, angrily, "Crack!" She denied it and seemed very angry that I would even ask. I started to feel bad again especially since I accused without evidence. Even though I apologized to her the damage was already done. We had been down this path before and it had always ended the same way. We were somehow able to get past the tension and continue the evening.

After a long day I was tired and looked forward to getting in the bed. I was glad for the change because on most nights Carol stayed out late and I found only a cold empty bed to accompany me to sleep. To my delight Carol had remained home and it felt like all was well. As I closed my eyes to drift into a peaceful rest, I was awakened suddenly by a loud frightful cry. The words "Oh no, what have I done!" pierced the fleeting stillness of my night. It was Carol's cries of remorse screaming from the other side of the bathroom door. Still half asleep and startled by the noise I struggled to make sense of what was happening. Trying to focus, I looked at the clock and it appeared to be a little past four o'clock in the morning. My moment of clarity was again interrupted as she kept repeating, "What have I done, what have I done"? I hurriedly ran to the shower only to find her standing in a pool of blood crying. Frantic, I said, "My God you're bleeding! What happened?" She moaned, "I was trying to get the baby out of me." Then she murmured something about taking some kind of home remedy to induce labor. So that's what she was out to get earlier, I thought. My heart sank. I ran to the phone to dial 911. Within a few minutes the ambulance came. I can remember the cold steel and sound of the fetal monitor as the baby's heart rate would slow down and speed up. I instantly started praying that it would be born healthy and safely. We were quickly rushed to the hospital to prepare for delivery. This was Carol's third child so the labor was short, and by the time we were in the delivery room the child was on its way out and that morning my first son, DeWayne Junior, was born. The doctors were very quiet as they reviewed his blood work. I quickly asked, "What's going on?" The doctor answered, "Your child is having difficulty because of a reactionary disease, a condition associated with premature infants." He then said, "This is not consistent with his current stage of development." "What does this mean concerning his ability to survive?" I questioned. He explained that it would be difficult and that he would try to get him through this very rough time. He went on to ask how things were going back at home. I explained that it had been kind of rough. He then proceeded to ask if we would have help with caring for the baby after we brought him home. He did everything but ask, "Are you aware that your child has been exposed to crack cocaine?" He ended the conversation with, " I need to turn the case over to a social worker for follow up. However as a favor to you, I'm telling you, you should get your family out of here before anyone else needs to read the lab reports."

I didn't say anything to Carol about it, I was far too angry and believed if I could just get him home and have him eat, everything would be all right. Carol was afraid for the child because he had refused to nurse from her. We informed the nurse and the doctor ended up prescribing several baby formulas, but none worked. DeWayne Junior (DJ) could not keep anything down and had already lost a good deal of weight—he was fading fast. It also wasn't helping that Carol would get angry each time he refused her milk. She would cry so sorrowfully and remorsefully. I questioned myself, Was there a way I could have prevented this? I went upstairs and brought the baby down to the living room and began to pray over him. As I prayed, I lifted him up to God and said, "Surely you can heal him." I dedicated him unto the Lord that night, after which I was lead to call my mother. So I called her believing all the more that I was being led by the Spirit of God. It was a good thing I did! After explaining everything to her she said, "Get some Pet Milk and mix it half and half with water." I did what I was told and gave it to our baby. It was like a switch was turned on and another one was turned off. As he drank the milk he stopped crying and was able to keep it down. Within days he was able to take the milk with regular formula. A miracle had happened and the doctors were amazed when we returned for his well-check visit. He had gained a good deal of weight and was on the right track to recovering. Once again I had been face-to-face with a crisis and with our loved ones alongside we saw God's hand help us overcome. Knowing that a change needed to be made after battling for our son's survival, Carol confided that she wanted to stop smoking and "stuff." I agreed to be there to support her and work it out. For a time the home front started to look good and hope seemed to have returned to the household. Although certain changes had been made, our relationship was steadily declining. Only a few months had passed, and in that time we had already experienced several occasions where Carol had stayed away all night and I had gone out looking for her, only to find her hanging out on the street smoking. There were times when I could not find her and we both knew the next day would be ugly. On one occasion she told me her cousin needed her to drive him somewhere and she would be gone for the weekend. I didn't believe her and would not let her go. I knew that she was smoking cigarettes but I was afraid she would start smoking crack again. At the time I believed she was clean and I didn't want to see her go through a relapse. I did my best to work with her and even tried to include her parents; their support was needed in the matter. It seemed like it was one thing after another with Carol even after reaching out to a rehab clinic to obtain help. Things started to look up again when she started to attend Sunday services with me. Dr. Patterson ,our pastor, had invited her to sing in the choir and we both thought it was a great idea. There was one song that I love to hear her sing, it was called, "Walk Around Heaven All Day." She had a beautiful voice and was soon asked to sing with a local group. When she mentioned the idea to me and asked if I minded if she joined. I readily agreed. I was equally curious about the opportunity and decided to go along with her to the practices. The group met at her mother's home every so often and rehearsed for several hours there. The group would always begin practice with their theme song, "Change." The song was about the transformation that takes place after one's salvation experience. The sad part about the matter was they would smoke cannabis before and after they would perform. At first they tried concealing it from me and when I suspected what was happening, I no longer attended practice. Carol continued to sing with them and although I talked with her about it, she only said what she believed I wanted to hear. After a while the group eventually dissolved and I continued in my efforts to work with her. I had decided to love Carol as long as she wanted to be with me. I wasn't going to leave her, even though we lead very different lives. After I came to the understanding of what a marriage covenant meant, I had hope for our relationship. However, it was only a few weeks after the beginning of the New Year, January 1988, that Carol left for the second time—leaving me with an empty home as I indicated at the start of this book. The memory of Carol's abdication of our marriage, which resulted in our son being torn from my life and me being left with nothing, didn't seem so bad now. The surplus of time proved useful and helped in developing a closer walk with God.

Now, here I was almost a year later, in December 1988, by the grace of God, and the anger I once carried had been exchanged for hope and expectation. Sorrow had been replaced with the joy of the Lord. I was no longer moved by the happenings in my life. Fear had been replaced by faith. No longer swayed by what I saw, I was now holding fast to the Word that I knew. It's something about God's refining process that will bring you forth in a newness of life.

Chapter 10:
Holding out for a Hero - her Tale

After Jacqui mailed me the "Dear John" letter, a whirl-wind of events took place in her life. As I shared earlier, when Jacqui and I parted ways that February in 1987, she returned to Birmingham. The first few weeks were very difficult for her in that she was wrestling with a guilty conscience. She had fallen in love with a married man, and although he was separated from his wife he was still very married. She was still asking herself how she could have allowed herself to do this. Of course, with this kind of mental anguish, her mother would notice.

Jacqui and her mother had a special kind of relationship. They were more than just mother and daughter. The long illness of her father, followed by his passing, served as a season for the two of them to become each other's primary support and friends. Jacqui became a backup for several aspects of her mother's many entrepreneurial ventures. Her mother was her number one cheerleader for her completing college. They both knew they could ask anything of the other and expect a best effort. When her mother relocated to Birmingham from Boston at the request of her ailing father, who was adamant that he did not want to die in Boston, her mother sold all of her businesses and housing complexes to grant him his wish. When asked by her mother to move to Alabama from Massachussetts, Jacqui surrendered her scholarship and took what she describes as the worst trip off her life. The greyhound bus ride from Boston to Birmingham was no cakewalk. She had no idea what to expect in Birmingham. That trip was the first time she had gone past New York City heading south. To say the least, Jacqui and her mother were close.

Her mother knew that she was out of sorts and asked her what was going on. So, she let it all out. After sharing her heart with her mother, her mother had these comforting words, "Jacqui you are doing the right thing. If you love a thing and let it go, if it's yours it will come back to you. If not it was not for you" To most, it would have been just another cliché, but for Jacqui it was enough for her to be on her way. Her mother, who had been a long-time business owner, decided that she no longer wanted the responsibility of the business and desired to return to Boston. Jacqui's mother asked her to go ahead of her to Boston to find an apartment and make preparation for the move while she closed her business. The timing of this move felt perfect for Jacqui. She had graduated from the University of Alabama at Birmingham three months earlier andstill had not found a job in in Social Work. Thus, the move to Boston was right on-time for her. Jacqui's pastor was not too happy about it because her work with drama ministry was excellent. She had recently completed a musical production of a play she had written and directed called, Judgment Day. It was a hit. Many individuals had come to salvation as a result of its message. Furthermore, the singles ministry at the church had been a great blessing to her. That's where she learned that it was the responsibility of single brothers and sisters in Christ to protect one another from hurtful relationships and prepare one another for healthy and wholesome relation-ships. She had friendships there and one male friend in particular treated her like a princess and taught her to expect kindness and honor from suitors. Nonetheless, her mother had asked her to scout out a place to live and she was more than ready to try something different—so she was off to Boston.

Jacqui stayaed with her sister Johnnie May while she was searching for a place. Although Jacqui had been raised in the city of Boston, there had been a major revitalization in the city that changed the layout and the demographics of various areas. She had known Boston to be a place that was relatively easy when it came to job search. Now, here she was a college graduate and was having the hardest time even getting a job interview. From her childhood she had maintained an unofficial philosophy that was born out of her endless walks to friends' homes and church, dreaming along the way, "The world is round and I'll eventually get there." However, life was changing and life's challenges required focus. She had to quickly learn that if you weren't being watchful you could easily become a victim. It was as if in the four short years they had been away, the city had spiraled into real estate bedlam and social chaos. The safe feeling once experienced while casually strolling along on one of her walks from Dorchester to Boston was completely gone. It was during the mid to late eighties when the crack cocaine and gang warfare was rampant. Once a place where one could find a few pockets of the wonderful life, Dorchester had become a dying oasis. The cost of living in Boston was exorbitant. Her car insurance cost more than the value of the car. Her mother had prepared her for a different world. As a teenager she was given the best clothing and told that she would live in the best places and travel the world and do great things. The world she returned to was different from what she had prepared for. There she was all dressed in a luxurious red wool coat trimmed in black, with black gloves and a black fur lined head wrap as if she was off to the Waldorf Astoria. Her southern polished presentation was fruitless in finding a job. Although the scenario wasn't so promising, she remained diligent in her efforts.

One afternoon her sister Johnnie overheard her trying to get an appointment for an interview and offered her this advice, "You need to talk to them." Jacqui thought to herself, Well isn't that what I'm doing? So she replied to Johnnie, "What do you mean?" Johnnie said, "You've got to express yourself, connect with them...you know...talk... be down to earth!" So Jacqui did just that. She removed the polish from her speech and spoke to the gatekeepers and hireing officials as if she had known them forever. By the end of that week not only had she gotten an interview but also she had a job and was now onto finding an apartment for her and her mother.

Chapter 11:
The Parade of Suitors

This was a different time for Jacqui. Unknowingly, she was about to run a gauntlet of sorts that would not only challenge her faith, but test her will to trust those closest to her. After getting the apartment, she began to settle into a daily routine. On one occasion, she was traveling home on the bus from work when this very dark, short and stocky male with the whitest teeth she had ever seen approached her. After seeing her ride the bus several times, he asked if he could speak to her. Now, she had not paid much attention to him other than an occasional nod of her head. Remembering where and who she was, she knew she had to stay on guard at all times. It was very important not to appear too approachable because she knew that the slightest eye contact could invite unwanted attention. While the city of Boston was known for its icy aloofness to strangers, the subculture on public transportation provided a venue for easy acquiantences. It was not uncommon to have group conversations and make acquaintance that could become life long friends. This guy did not appear to be threatening and they were on the bus. Her assumption was right, it turned out that he was a Christian and wanted to know if she attended weeknight church services. His name was Sean. He was a minister and thought that she might be interested in joining him at a special missionary fundraising concert. She politely turned him down but he gave her his number and she promised to call him. Well as it turns out, her church group was participating in the same service. She and the minister talked after service. He told her more about his family's ministry. She was intrigued about the missionary work and his life before he came to America. They were in fact missionaries from Nigeria to America. She wanted to meet his family to find out more about what they were doing, so she gave him her number. The next day he called and invited her to meet his sister. His sister greeted her with the same enthusiastic smile that seemed to say, "You are the most important person in the world to me right now." She was courteous and answered Jacqui's many questions about ministry, missionary work and Nigeria. Sean interrupted their conversation and asked to speak to Jacqui alone. Once alone, he was very direct in saying, "I believe you are supposed to be my wife." Jacqui quickly replied, "I don't think so, perhaps friends." He said, "No, I need a wife and I feel you should give me a chance." But Jacqui was emphatic about her feelings. She explained that she would not marry a minister and that she was not in a place in her life for a relationship. He pursued for several weeks but she remained steadfast in her response. Well that was it for the short yet eventful moment of them being "together."

Jacqui was settling into being back home in Boston. She felt comfortable again walking the streets of Dorchester. She loved looking at the various styles of houses. One street could host numerous styles of homes— two stories, three stories, Capes, Victorians and Colonials, all decorated to reflect the personality of the owner. Most houses were trimmed with white or tan, but the house colors reflected the rainbow. It was spring in Boston, her favorite time to walk about. The washer/dryer at her home was on the fritz, so she walked to the local laundry mat. On one occasion while doing her laundry, another suitor's eye fell upon her. I'm sure by now you are wondering if she had "marry me" tattooed on her forehead. The answer is no, she did not. Nonetheless, it seemed as if everywhere she went she caught the eye of someone. In fact, she had only been to the laundry a few times. In spite of her infrequent presence, a young man immediately noticed her. As she was waiting for her clothes to complete their cycle, she could feel someone looking at her. As she looked around to discover who was watching her, their eyes met. At first, she took his gaze to be a chance glance. So naturally, she returned to tending to her laundry. Moments later she noticed someone sitting on the washer next to her quietly waiting. When she looked up, he smiled and with a slight Irish brogue asked, "Who might I have the pleasure of meeting?" She immediately recognized the accent from some very unpleasant childhood memories. She thought, My goodness, things have really changed since then. This white guy from South Boston (A part of Boston where blacks were very rarely found.) is here talking to me. How am I supposed to handle this kind of situation? Now to an outsider this may not seem to be anything of interest, but to someone reared in the self-segregated city of Boston in the '60s and '70s it was. Looking up at him, she was intrigued by the novelty of the matter. He offered to get her something warm to drink as there was a slight chill in the air. Then, of course, Jacqui's proof-of-true-Christian-faith questions began. As usual, the questions continued until she felt it might be safe to allow this person into her life. In the midst of all the questions she learned that the guy's name was Matthew Burgess. She decided she would take him up on that cup of coffee if he were still offering it. As they made their way to the coffee shop only a few blocks away, she could not help looking around to check if anyone was staring. She learned much about him that day. He was a kind person working to support a missionary in the Philippines. I should add that this gentleman was quite the opposite of the earlier suitor. He was tall, not quite as direct, and his spirit did not seem as hardened by the ravages of a war. However, he too, had an accent as he spoke. He said very gently, "You're new 'round here aren't you? I see you leave and go, to what I think is work, dressed real well. When you come home you do not have a lot of stuff going on." At first she thought, Has he been stalking me? Then she asked, "Why do you know so much about me?" He replied, "I'm a people watcher and I'm your neighbor." People watching was a popular pastime in the city. She knew that some people just kind of hung out and watched people simply because people can be fascinating. As he went on quietly sharing his experiences, she thought, Wow! He's cute and a Christian! He's white and Irish, but I suppose we might be friends if we are willing to risk our lives. For her it was quite the new experience. Until the time she left to go to the South, the Irish and Blacks did not really talk or get along very well at all. In fact, as a youth who walked the city regularly, she would explain the invisible color division lines to newcomers, hoping to protect them from getting hurt by accidently crossing the wrong street at the wrong time of day. Can you imagine? There she was in a public place chatting with a blond-haired, blue-eyed man. He raved about how sweet she seemed. Jacqui thought, laying aside all her emotions, This man is nice, he is kind, he is charming and he seems sweet enough, but he's not the one for me. In her heart, it was pleasant to know that someone was pleased by her presence, but she knew Matthew was not the one for her. That being said, his efforts to woo her were destined to fail. After a couple of month's of spending casual time together. She said at that time she was not really looking for anyone, and he understood. Then she said, "It does not mean we can't be friends," and gently encouraged him to redirect his romantic efforts elsewhere.

Chapter 12:
Heavenly Hearing…Pray and Obey

Soon the days turned to weeks and weeks to months, during this time Jacqui turned her attention to the work of the church. She and her mother had settled into an apartment not far from her job and she now had free time. Why not reengage with church? She had been very active with church family at More Than Conquerors Faith Church in Birmingham, Alabama. Being the radical that she was, she didn't want to forget the lover of her soul who was Jesus Christ. On this one Saturday, her pastor had invited a missionary out of Africa to speak; it was the summer of 1988. Bishop Coker was a co-laborer of Bishop Benson Idahosa, a renowned missionary in the area. After he had spoken, he held an alter call for all the singles. He made this statement, "If you are single, over 24, have completed college, are not given to celibacy, you need to be married. Come down here, I'm going to pray for you and you will be married within the next year." It was an open invitation to participate in a prophetic proclamation. Jacqui met all of the requirements except for one. She had no desire to be married. The Bishop continued to entreat the reticent audience explaining that it was God's responsibility to do the match making and that if he had to send people all across the world to be joined, he would do it. He also admonished the singles that it was their responsibility to marry, not to just date around; their obligation was to obey the Word of the Lord that was spoken. With that said, almost all of the single adults in the audience, including herself, went to the alter for prayer. The Bishop prayed, anointed them, and they all went on with their lives. In Jacqui's case, things seem to get very busy all of a sudden. The commitment to her job began to encroach into her personal time. Since she was spending the bulk of her time at work, the community health center, she wanted it to feel as much like home as possible, so she was always trying to move something in or out of her office. This constant moving required assistance from, Al, the janitor who seemed to be a nice guy. As a matter of fact when she needed someone to help move furniture for her or her mother he gladly assisted. He soon became a common fixture of sorts in her life. Somehow he was just there and seemed to be a good man and a nice friend to have until he asked her out to dinner. At first, it was simple and to Jacqui—he was just a nice guy. Al was from the Bahamas. He met about forty percent of her checklist for a suitable mate. He was tall, dark and handsome, he could work with his hands and he wasn't a minister. So when he asked her to consider marrying him she was seriously considering it. Remembering the prayer that the Bishop had prayed concerning marriage, she thought that perhaps he was the one. Because their relationship started merely as a simple friendship, Al slipped in under the radar of what I call the "Jacqui Fake-Christian Detection System" or "JFCDS." Because of this she would spend a lot of time wrestling with the Holy Spirit regarding the sincerity of his Christian conversion. To help resolve this matter she invited him to church to see how he would fit in. One Sunday morning she slipped into the back of the church for service late with Al and left early hoping no one would really notice them as she was not quite ready to introduce him to her Christian friends or the church leaders.

On the next Sunday after service, the pastor called Jacqui aside and proceeded to tell her that the guy she was with was not "the one" and to leave him alone. Jacqui was stunned. She did not understand how the pastor even saw her in a crowd of over five hundred people. She had purposely sat in the back to the side, out of the pastor's direct line of sight. She told me that she knew in her spirit that he was not right for her, but he had grown on her. She liked his family and enjoyed the aroma of Bajan food being cooked by his sister when she visited. Not wanting to hurt him, she thought how she might break the news to him gently. One day he suddenly presented her an engagement ring to which she responded, "This kind of thing requires much thought and real time." This was a nice way of saying, "I'm not sure and I need to consult with those who are not blinded by infatuation like my mother, or somebody I can trust to hear from God." She remembered the words of the pastor and she could not keep laying them aside. She knew that for the blessing of the Lord to be upon you, one must always give honor to one's parents and those who have rule over you. That was one thing about Jacqui, she really tried to learn from others and worked meticulously to make as few mistakes as possible. That might seem a bit archaic but sometimes the old way is the best way. Well, after consulting with her mother and sister Betty Rose, they advised her to take a vacation to South Carolina. Now, I should mention that her mother didn't say yea or nay, she simply started to pray about the entire matter. When Jacqui arrived in South Carolina, she met with her cousins and spent the time enjoying the scenery. On Wednesday of that week she decided to look into employment opportunities in the area. By that Friday, she had a job and an apartment. That was unheard of at that time—to go into a city and have such success was a testament to the power of prayer. A loving mother's prayer and a God move hookup!

Now when she returned to Boston she was a little surprised at her mother's instructions, "Do not see this man, Al, again, and do not call or contact this man anymore either. Pack all of your belongings, rent a U-Haul, and ask one of the brothers from the church to drive you to South Carolina." Although she did not understand the no-contact edict from her mother, she followed her instructions exactly. After spending a few minutes on the phone, she had a U-Haul and shortly after she had a driver who happened to be a longtime friend and member of the church. Stealing away in secrecy under the cloak of darkness was surreal to her. It was difficult because she felt like she was running away although she was not quite sure why. However, she knew that obedience was better than sacrifice. So she obeyed her mother.

The drive was almost like therapy. The conversations were long and filled with hope and the dream of the two young minds. She discovered that her long-time friend had a dream of completing college, and hers was to actually go on the missionary field. Their conversation seemed to make the drive time pass quickly. She realized that for the first time in her life she would be on her own with her very own apartment and because her old car died she bought a brand new car. To her, this would be the beginning of a wonderful journey.

Chapter 13:
On Her Own

For Jacqui it didn't take much for her to settle into her new apartment. She was excited about diverting from the lavish childhood home experiences of formal dining and living rooms with chandlers and fancy furniture. She was really quite happy about having only three pieces of furniture with a simple fireplace and a newly acquired skill of starting a real fire in it. She was carefree and as happy as could be. As a child, life had dealt her some pretty rough cards that taught her to love every day that God allows you to live healthy. In understanding accountability to God, it only took a short while to realize that if she did not become more focused on her life's goals; she was not going to get anywhere. She turned her attention to finding a good church home and spending time in prayer with Christ, the lover of her soul. She spent many evenings driving the roads, learning the area and enjoying the changing of the autumn colors over the hilly landscape. As she began to look at all that God had done and was doing in her life, she began to ponder about her purpose and placement. She spent a lot of time praying about where she was supposed to be and what she was to be doing to serve God. Her cousin knew that she had no friends in the area, so she introduced her to a co-worker, Burros. He was, as her mother would say, "Something good for looking." He was tall, about six foot two inches, with a slight resemblance to Denzel Washington. Along with being handsome and well-educated, he was in the same career as Jacqui, Social Work. He had it all with one exception, he was a minister and pastor of a local church. Therefore, he was automatically disqualified from her list of potentials for marriage. Besides, after all their talking and getting to know each other, he had never really expressed any interest of the romantic kind toward her. She and Burros would spend hours talking on the phone. He was from the Islands and his accent was a familiar sound that often made her feel at home. She felt safe having Bible discussions with someone where, in her mind, romance was not an option. They even spent Thanksgiving together and agreed that simple friendship worked for them.

She purposed in her heart to continue to fall more in love with Jesus. In doing so she longed to spend time in the missionary field. She wanted to put to use some of the training she had received from Mother Watson, a traveling missionary in the Church of God in Christ. Jacqui was inspired by her diligence and spiritual power through prayer and believed she was ready to carry the standard. While in Alabama she had been fortunate to meet a missionary from Jamaica. She remembered that she had her business card and decided to contact her. The missionary's reply was very enthusiastic to say the least. However, Jacqui's enthusiasm was clouded by the missionary's remarks about the abundance of available male preachers on the island, which put a bit of a damper on her desire to move quickly to the mission field in Jamaica or any field.

Jacqui had been active in the local church she was attending and had free time, so she decided to remove any opportunity to slip into idleness by taking a part-time job at one of her favorite restaurants, Steak & Ale. She enjoyed the warm atmosphere and was thankful for her wallet's sake to have free access to the salad bar.

Chapter 14:
Heavenly Reconnection, God's Divine Messenger

Life was wonderful for Jacqui and her world was filled with more than enough. She had purposed in her heart to rise early for meditation and prayer. By the grace of God she was doing quite well. It was tantamount to an act of God for Jacqui to routinely rise earlier than necessary before work. She was definitely not a morning person. As a child, waking her in the morning became that of a ritual of sorts. Her mother would call to her, "Jacqui wake up dear! Wake now the day is getting away." As I said earlier, she was there for her mom and her mom was there for her. I suppose the Holy Spirit started to fill-in for her mom when it came to waking her in the morning. I believe when the songwriter wrote, "The Lord woke me up this morning and strated me on my way," he was writing it for Jacqui. As with most of us, time seems to speed up when we are enjoying ourselves because before she realized it the holiday season was upon her. By that time, she had grown accustomed to her early morning interludes with the Holy Ghost. It was not uncommon for her to be awakened by that wonderful still voice with instructions for the day. She would pray about and receive instructions on things like what to wear, how to speak, and what to pray about.

On one morning she believed that she had received a notion to call me. That troubled her greatly for an entire day. You see, she thought that she heard in her spirit to, Call DeWayne's mom. It was troubling because the prompting came suddenly without warning and was in conflict with what she believed was God's will. She felt she was being tested as she had been trying to practice complete obedience to the promptings of the Holy Spirit. Jacqui dismissed the prompting believing it to be the residual from a love that was long past and could never be. She was angry with herself much of the day for even having the thought and was in a continuous internal debate about where the idea even came from. The following morning was Christmas. That night she went to sleep watching the fire in the fireplace die out. Suddenly, early, before the light of day, a great brightness entered into her room and woke her with a loud voice saying emphatically, "Call DeWayne's mother!" Startled awake by this holy cacophony, her heart still pounding and racing in her chest, she sprang up in her bed. Confused, frustrated, and seeking clarity, without really thinking, she implored the Holy Spirit, "Why did DeWayne marry the wrong person?" Quicker than she ever imagined possible, the Holy Spirit promptly replied, "He made a mistake." After this brief tete-a-tete with God, she acquiesced and agreed to do as told. It is important that you understand that this was taking place without me have any knowledge of it at all. I was in Century, Florida, waiting for a call that I believed only God could initiate. And I might add, I thought that Jacqui was still living in Boston, Massachusetts. However, I did know this much, for Jacqui to call me, it would require God's divine intervention. She had made me well aware of her difficulties in recalling information about people. But on this occasion God did something special. She remembered my mother's name, the name of my hometown and my mom's address, after meeting my mother only once. Listen to this, she also had to fight against her logic and her belief that by now I had relocated to Japan with

80

Carol. Even with all of these very real possibilities, she had faith to obey what she felt was clear direction from the Holy Spirit and believed God for His will to be done.

Jacqui later shared with me that as the operator began to read the number to her, an intense emotional flood of memories filled her mind. A thousand "What ifs," such as Chief saying, "Baby, he's not here, he has moved to Japan," or "?Jacqui who?" After speaking to herself, she quieted the murmurings of her soul. Sometimes you have to say hush to your mind because if not, it will run wild, carrying you with it. It is in those moments that our faith is tried and the discipline of obedience is tested. She held it together and was able to dial the numbers. Sitting on the edge of her bed she awaited the answer on the other end of the ringing phone. With every ring her heart fluttered in fear that there would be no answer or possibly even worse, it would be answered.

I had answered the phone several times that morning, as it was the tradition to call home on Christmas if you could not be there. When the phone rang with the third call that Christmas morning, I answered, in my radio greeting voice, "Thomas residence, Merry Christmas." I was still expecting another family member to be on the other end. I paused, and then there was this sound that I had not heard for close to a year. It was a sweet sound, one that I had been waiting on with all anticipation and hope, believing God to do His work.

It was her reply to my greeting, so simple and meek, "DeWayne?" With boldness I sang to her, "You are my wife", in the melody of the Green Acres sitcom intro. I quickly shared with her the events of the past forty-eight hours and how I had prayed after calling Boston and failing to reach her. I prayed and asked God, "If she is my wife please have her call me." Now, I want you to know that we had spoken only for a few minutes before Jacqui asked if my divorce from my first wife was final. My reply was that in February all would be final. You see, in the state of Mississippi there is a one-year waiting period before the final divorce decree can be issued by the court. It turns out I still had two months to go. The decree wouldn't be final until the fifteenth of February 1989. To which she said, "I will have to say goodbye for now. I can't really have anything to do with you until the divorce is final." I knew it would have been futile to say anything other than, "Very well, I look forward to that day when we will be free to choose our destiny." She said, "Bye now." I replied, "I love you." We quietly hung up our phones. Chief was lying there and heard the entire exchange. Her response was textbook faith. She said, "Just like the Lord had her call you, He can put you two together." Well, her words were nice, but I wanted and needed more. What I didn't know is that God was planning to show me how to be patient and how to let patience do its perfect work.

Chapter 15:
Looking For God's "Do" on Her Fleece

I'd like to share something with you that Jacqui would only reveal later in our restored relationship, her fleecing of God. The concept of "putting out a fleece" comes from the story of Gideon, a leader in Israel. The story can be found in the sixth chapter of Judges. For Jacqui the situation that was unfolding required divine clarity. In her mind, there still was the matter that I was going to be divorced, so she really wanted to make sure this was right in God's eyes. On the same morning, after hanging up the phone with me, she went to her dining room table, sat down, took out her pen and on a piece of paper began to write a fleece before God. "Dear Father, I only want to do what is pleasing in your eyes. If this man is to be my husband these are the things that I need to see happen." Then she paused and thought of the prayer she had prayed so many times from her youth (She had always wanted to be married but she was very specific about her expectations), "Lord, prepare the man that is to be my husband, the one you have chosen from the foundation of the world to be my husband." Then she would pray, "Lord help me to be suitable adaptable and completing for him." She carefully wrote the following items concerning me and my life:

1. He needs to be accepted and blessed by my mother
2. He needs to be blessed by my pastors.
3. He needs to be free from alimony.
4. He needs to have no legal or financial issues.
5. He needs to be baptized in the Holy Ghost speaking in other tongues.

6. He needs to be free from financial ties to ex-wife, no joint property.
7. He needs to have complete custody of his son.

She then took the note and taped it to the back of her refrigerator. She told no one about it. She had decided in her heart that she would not marry me if the things on the list did not happen.

Chapter 16:
A Financial Hook Up

After that phone call, I must say my faith was increased ever the more. Just look at what just happened before my eyes. If there was ever a modern day "and suddenly" this was one of them. I had tried to reach Jacqui on my own and was quite unsuccessful, and then by the grace of God He divinely inspired her to call me at my mother's home. I mean God did it! All I had to do was just be patient and have faith. Well, my mother's health sprang forth like the morning, and by the first of the year she was getting around and was returning to her old routine. I felt blessed that the Lord had allowed me to be a part of her recovery, and was comfortable returning to Biloxi to work.

I was going about my daily tasks and dealing with the many troubles that my first wife had left behind. On one occasion while finishing up for the day, I received a phone call that shook me to my core. Someone had transferred the call to my suite. The phone rang and I answered, "This is Staff Sergeant DeWayne Thomas, how may I help you?" The male voice on the other end replied with a Mississippi drawl,, "Son, you can come on down here or we can come out there and get you boy." I said, "May I ask who this is?" The voice replied, "This is the Jefferson County Sheriff's Department." My heart started to pound rapidly within my chest. I respectfully asked, "May I ask where you are located?" The voice replied, "This is the Jefferson County Sheriff's Department." I jotted down on a note pad the address he proceeded to give me. I quickly asked, "Why do you want to see me?" He replied, "I'm not at liberty to discuss this over the phone. You need to get on down here now!" And with that he hung up the phone. Not sure what to do next I ran to my supervisor and informed him of my situation. He promptly relieved me of duty and advised me to keep him informed and let him know if I needed help. I thought to myself, What did he mean 'If I needed help,' didn't he hear what I had said? I'm on my way to turn myself in for something and I don't even know why!

I went straight to the courthouse; my heart was racing and palms sweating. Needless to say, I was terrified. I was not sure what charges were going to be filed against me. When I arrived at the courtroom the sheriff explained to me that he had papers to serve me. He further explained that I would need to go before the judge if I could not pay off all the bad checks I had written. My first thought was, How could this be? You see, I had dealt with this matter earlier. Back in September I had gone home to my bank, and had spoken with a former employer; a family friend, JR. JR had a written affidavit stating that the signatures on the checks had been forged and that no one was to accept any check in my name unless I was physically present with a valid ID. After my brief mental excursion about the past, I asked how much was owed. The officer said "$30,000." Oh Lord $30,000? I don't have that kind of money! I thought. The sheriff walked out of the room. After a few minutes he returned with the judge who then asked me to step up to the bench. He read the charges and asked if I had anything to say. I replied, "Your Honor I did not write the checks. My ex-wife wrote them!" The judge then asked, "When did she become your ex-wife?" I replied, "Our divorce will be final February of 1989." The judge said, "Then everything that happens after that date will be her problem, but you sir were still married and had not filed for the divorce when about $15,000 were spent and therefore you are responsible." I asked,"Why? I did not write them." He replied, "In Mississippi, we have something called Joint Tenancy Law, which means while you are married fifty percent of any assets or liabilities are divided equally between the two married parties. When that debt is unpaid they hold whomever they can find liable." After everything sunk in and I was able to wrap my brain around what had just happened I nearly fell to the floor. Where was I going to get that kind of money? And to top it all off, the judge said I had to have it by the following Monday or I would find myself in jail. I was in a stupor. Dazed and somewhat disoriented I made my way to the church. I don't know why, but I thought, if I could get to the church maybe the pastor could help me sort things out.

Sure enough my pastor was there, and being a lawyer he was able to advise me that I really should take this matter seriously for two reasons: One, he said this kind of thing is a felony and it has the potential to follow me the rest of my life. Two, pointing to the paper, he said it could hurt your potential to be ordained or even keep your licenses as an African Methodist Episcopal (AME) Deacon. Man, that made me feel terrible. Here I had spent two years of my life in the seminary and it was all about to come to an end. The ramification of how detrimental the matter was had finally started to sink in. I knew this matter would require much prayer and faith. I knew that the pastor didn't have that kind of money lying around in an account. I thanked my pastor, left the church and went to my dorm.

There I began to pray and the Lord began to lead me by my Spirit to get the copies of the affidavits and take them to the grocery chain's management office. The charges had been brought against me by a large southern chain grocery store. I was hopeful that we could come to some kind of agreement on reducing the amount of money I was liable for. Leaving the dorm I made my way to the head store and asked to speak to the manager. The assistant manager informed me that the store manager was out of the office and that he would not be available. It is important that you know that when I presented the affidavit to the store's management the first time, they refused to speak with me. The only person who seemed the slightest bit concerned for me was the secretary who had a speech impediment or a very limited speaking ability. After watching me try desperately to speak with the store manager, the Spirit of the Lord moved on her; the same woman who had greeted me earlier and could barely speak clearly, was now speaking very clearly. She tapped me on the shoulder and said, "Here is the cell phone number of the regional director. You should give him a call. He might be able to help you." I took this miracle, of the clerk speaking clearly, as a sign that God was in the midst and that something great was about to transpire. The Word of God commands us to watch and pray. At the time I was watching and praying for any sign that God was there.

Prayerfully I took the number home to my dorm room and made the call. I was able to reach the gentleman and share my situation, and explained that there was an urgent need for attention and resolution. I needed all of this to happen by Monday morning to keep from being sent to jail. The director was amiable to hearing my entire story. Now to my surprise he said, "I will be in the area this weekend during which time I will give this matter my fullest attention." Well that was it; I had done all that I could do. The rest was now totally in the hands of the Lord. I prayed, "Lord you said 'Cast your cares upon me for I care for you.' Now then by faith I cast my cares upon you dear Lord." That was it, now the only thing left to do was keep my faith, wait, and be very patient.

I went about the rest of the weekend doing my normal tasks. I can remember at about three o'clock in the morning I was troubled in my sleep. My mind was racing with "What If" questions. I had to wrestle my mind back under control and I began to pray for the Lord to help me. Soon a peace came over me and I fell asleep. Before long Monday morning was upon me and I woke up thinking to myself, What should I do? Should I go to work as usual or report to the courthouse?

After much consternation I elected to go to work and continue to let God handle it. I had been at work for nearly an hour when the front desk paged me to pick up the phone. I ran to the phone and to my surprise, the voice on the other end was the regional director for the grocery chain. He promptly informed me that all charges had been dropped. I was cleared of all criminal charges, and the responsibility for the debt was no longer mine. They had agreed to print a retraction in the local newspaper. I expressed my gratitude for him taking the time to look into the matter and hung up the phone. Words can't express the jubilation in my heart at the time. I had to get away to praise my God. I shouted, "Thank you Lord!" I then fell to the floor and weeping with joy I praised my Father in Heaven. I just had to go and tell somebody, the only person I could think of was my supervisor, my military mentor. At the end of the day I went to my church board meeting and testified of the hand of God to the brothers and sisters of my church family. I had received a financial and legal hookup and had been delivered from a thirty thousand dollar financial debt along with clean record and a cleared name! Little did I know, the Lord was working on Jacqui's fleece list one item at a time.

Chapter 17:
God's Parental Hookup

My financial hook up was just one of the many miracles that were to take place between the time Jacqui and I were brought together by phone that Christmas morning and the time we would be married. I'd like to share all of my Heavenly hook ups but I will note the ones that warrant special attention.

Now, it was around the last week of January, and I was on my way to work when someone called out my name in an apparent attempt to get my attention. I turned around to see who it might be. It was Chris, a friend of mine from the dorm. I had come to know him through his photography. He helped me put together my courting pictures to send to Jacqui. Seeing that she and I had not seen each other for almost a year, I thought it might not be a bad idea to send her my current image in pictures. I went over to see what he wanted. I asked what I could do for him. His reply seemed a bit odd—his girlfriend wanted to see me at his room that afternoon. I thought to myself, Why she would want to see me at his room? I laughed and said, "Hey dude, I'm not into …" He raised his hands to interrupt me, "It's not like that." I smiled and asked, "Well what is it?" He said, "Just trust me and be there." I agreed to be there and I walked off wondering what in the world his girlfriend had to talk to me about.

After struggling to get through the day, wondering about the purpose of my evening appointment, I hastily made my way to Chris' dorm room. His girlfriend was there. I was keenly focused on discovering the purpose of our meeting. As I stood quietly, her voice interrupted the silence as she advised me that I should probably sit down before she shared her urgent message. I sat on the edge of the bed as she began by asking a series of questions, "Are you DeWayne Thomas?" I replied, "Yes." Then she asked, "Do you have a son?" I answered again, "Yes." Interrupting her, I asked, "Is everything alright?" Not fazed by the intensity of my response she said, "About a week ago, your ex-wife Carol asked my mother if she would watch little DJ while she went downtown to pick up some diapers and a few other items. But when my mother agreed, Carol didn't return that day or that night for that matter. The next day we started searching for her and we were unsuccessful. DeWayne, it has been several days and we have not heard from her. I mentioned the situation to Chris and he said he knew a Staff Sergeant Thomas but wasn't sure if it was you." I was blown away at first. What was I expected to do? How was I going to handle this? Then it came to me, Maybe this is how I am to get DeWayne Jr. back. Yes, I remembered the Lord had promised me that he would give my son back to me. As I came to myself I quickly asked for her parents address and phone number. She gave me an envelope with the address written on it as I stood up. I told her thank you and quickly left his room. Racing to the phone, I could only think of one person to call. Then everything seemed to slow down around me. I could hear my heart racing, with each beat it became louder. I could tell that I was running but each step felt like a minute was passing by. Whoa I thought! I'd better stop before I passed out. I stopped for a moment to steady myself and leaned against the wall. I was light headed. I knew it was my blood pressure. It had plagued me most of my adult life. After the faint feeling left, I made my way slowly to the phone.

I called my mother, Chief. I thought maybe she might have some advice on what I could do about this situation. After reaching her I blurted out, "Chief, she has abandoned DJ!" Chief responded, "Who did what? Who is this? Boy, is this you DeWayne?" Tearfully I replied,"Yes ma'am, it's me." "My how the mighty had fallen." There I was a grown man sobbing like a child. It is true, you do not want to be humbled by God! Years before after introduced Carol to momma she said the two of us didn't fit. We talked for ten minutes about the situation. Her words were comforting and full of faith. She told me that the Lord is working it all out, and somehow I would be able to go and get that baby and bring him to her. The entire matter overwhelmed me. But it was God keeping His word. Here I was broke, without a car and without any money to get a car. My credit had been destroyed because of the check forgeries. In spite of it all we agreed that it would all work out. I felt safe talking it through. At that moment just having someone to talk to made all the difference. Earlier I had felt as though no one could understand. I was supposed to be a strong man and there I was, on the phone crying like a baby to my mother. As I tried to focus on the encouraging words of my mother, I felt a sudden urge to end the conversation. The desire to end the call made no sense to me as I was enjoying the call and being comforted. As the urge continued to well up in the pit of my stomach I managed to blurt out, "Ok Chief, I'll let you know what happens." I broke down with tears and hung up the phone. It was only a few steps from the phone to my dorm room but it felt like the longest walk ever. I knew that some of my friends standing around heard the conversation and me crying. I can remember the fellows asking if I was all right. But I was spent; I didn't have any words to say. I just continued walking towards my room and closed the door behind me. I looked around, gazing at the small pieces of life I had been trying to hold close. I looked up to Heaven and cried out, "Lord I need you to…" And right about then I was interrupted by a yell from the hall. One of the guys had yelled, "Hey Doc! Hey Doc! You have a phone call, and it's a girl!" Now, I didn't really receive calls, let alone calls from any girls. As I raced towards the door to get to the phone I wondered who could it be. I had not given my number to anyone, at least not to any girls that I knew of. I picked up the phone and answered. The voice on the other end of the phone said, "It's me Jacqui." I couldn't believe it. It was Jacqui. I asked her, "Where are you?" She replied, "I'm in Mobile, Alabama, on my way to see you." I said, "Thank God! You don't know how much you are needed right now!" I explained to her that I was just on the phone and that something had moved me to get off the phone not more than five minutes ago. I asked her, "What made you come to see me?" She said the Holy Spirit had moved on her strongly to go to Mississippi during her morning prayer. She said the Lord told her that I needed her help. So trusting the Holy Spirit, she called into her job and advised them that she had some personal business that she needed to take care of. Then she said, "I started driving and praying." She traveled through the entire day and into the stormy night. Later I learned that this was a feat in itself. You see, Jacqui has poor night vision and is terribly afraid of lightning, but somehow God helped her through it all. She continued to say, "When I arrived in Mobile, Alabama I stopped and called the base locater to find your phone number. I needed to find out where you were staying." At that point I just began thanking God and I finally stopped long enough to give her instructions on where to meet me. I figured she was about an hour and a half away from the base, so at about midnight I went to the gate to await her arrival and to sign her in.

It was around 12:10 in morning when she arrived. She pulled in driving a new car, a little red Plymouth Sundance. When she step out of the car it was obvious that she had rushed to get here. She seemed a bit tired, but after she had gotten over the shock of my weight loss, slowly that beautiful smile that had captured me before returned. I welcomed it, it was warming—she was my Jacqui. We chatted for awhile as I got her to lodging.

The next day we met up for breakfast and talked about what would be the best way to go and get DJ. As we were reacquainting ourselves, she acknowledged that this trip was contrary to her plan to not have any contact with me prior to the finalized divorce. But it appeared that God had something else planned. Jacqui later shared with me that there was a flood of emotions around every step of this trip, but none so great as when she first held little DJ in her arms.

When we arrived, DJ was dirty and hungry and they had him in what appeared to be a makeshift diaper. Everything within Jacqui just wanted to get him to a place where he could feel safe, clean and warm. It was a long drive to my hometown and what little money I had went towards paying for the gas. I wondered if Chief had recovered well enough from her cancer surgery to care for little DJ. I mean, I knew she was doing well enough to take care of herself and Tess but what about DJ, he was just a baby. I just put it all aside and tried to enjoy the ride and getting to know Jacqui again.

As I drove us to my mother's home in Century, we talked about the many things that had transpired since had last been together. We talked about our triumphs and failures and everything in between. In a few hours we were there. My mother was waiting with great anticipation for our arrival. She made a special breakfast for DJ. Grits, eggs, toast and everything you can imagine in a country breakfast was the order of the day.

Jacqui and I went to the Dollar Store and picked up as many supplies as we could. She used her credit card and I went to the bank to withdraw some cash to leave with mom to help out. Although DeWayne Junior was in my custody, it was still a matter of the court's decision. While shopping I had a flash back of a conversation with my pastor. The conversation was regarding the promise that God made about me getting my son back. I remember him telling me that in the state of Mississippi a mother would have to abandon her child on the top of a telephone pole for seven days before losing custody. Jacqui did not know about my conversation with the pastor, nor did I know about her fleece to God for me to have full custody of my son, But God knew it all.

Jacqui asked if I would help her drive part of the way back to South Carolina. She was tired and still had to go to work the next day. I agreed not really thinking about how I would get myself back to Mississippi. Nonetheless, I set out to drive her at least to Montgomery, Alabama. The drive was so easy that before we realized it, we were almost in Birmingham. Once there, we went to the Greyhound bus terminal to get my ticket back to Mississippi. The cashier said it was $19 and some change. So, we returned to the car and began gathering up all the spare change lying around. We were able to come up with $15. We returned to the ticket clerk and asked if she could give us a military discount. Her reply was surprisingly quick and short; she looked up and said no, and without saying another word she looked back down to attend to her paperwork. So we returned to the car to keep looking for any ungathered change. While looking throughout the car a stranger had walked over to the car and was trying to get our attention. Jacqui said, "Dear, I think he wants something from us." I rolled down the window and asked what I could do for him. He replied, "I need money to get me something to eat." I looked at Jacqui and she looked at me and without a word we gave the old man a five-dollar bill. We knew that it was going to take more than those $15 we had to get me back to Biloxi, so we might as well help him out. We asked him to wait just a moment while we gather some more change for him. We looked down and gathered the rest of the loose change to give him as well. When we looked up after gathering the change, he was gone. I stepped out of the car to look around for the man but he was nowhere to be seen. It had only been a few seconds. We were parked in front of the old terminal next to the long wall it was a safe block. There were no nearby alleys. There were no buses. The terminal was empty. I know that it was physically impossible for this old man to run the length of the wall in 2 or 3 seconds. So we sat there for a moment and thought, How could he have disappeared? Perhaps it was an angel. We laughed. We were not sure, however, we decided to go back inside the terminal. The same sales person was still there and she beckoned for us to come to the window, so Jacqui approached her and she said that she didn't know why but she wanted to help us out. With that statement she sold me the ticket for $10. We thanked her for her kindness. Then we returned to our car rejoicing and praising God. It was a few hours before the next bus to Biloxi and while we were sitting there I was led to look under the seat and there was a folded up a ten-dollar bill that we had not seen in our earlier scavenge. Wow! Talk about a quick return of sowing in faith. I was now able to get something to eat and some reading material. We spent a few more minutes talking about Word of God and His faithfulness to watch over us. It soon came time for her to leave. I held her before exiting the car and watched her drive off, heading back to South Carolina.

As I boarded the bus to Biloxi I was so ready, it was 10 p.m., and sleep was hot and heavy on my trail. The buses were all delayed due to the poor weather conditions. The ride was long and seemed as if it would never end. As the bus approached Biloxi it was like the sky had open up to pour out all the rain in the heavens. I mean it was pouring down and I had only $2 to get from the bus station to the base. After I arrived at the Biloxi terminal, I got off the bus and flagged down a cab. When I got in I informed the driver that I only had $2 in my pocket and he nodded his head and we started out. I kept a close eye on the meter; I didn't want to go over what I had. The meter jumped to $1.35 almost instantly and after a few blocks it was registering $1.85. I was just about to say stop and let me out when the favor of God showed up. The driver reached over, turned the meter off and said, "I've seen you before. You are out preaching in the streets a lot around here. This one is on me." When we reached the gate I thought he would put me out but he insisted on driving me to the dorm's courtyard, literally to my front door. Man, talk about the favor of God!

After that last ordeal I said to God, "Lord you know I need a car but I really don't have a lot of money. It would be nice if you helped me so that I can drive back and forth to finish up my schooling with the church." After my prayer, I pretty much left it in God hands. The next day I overheard the guys talking about where they had gotten a really great deal on a car. I figured it wouldn't hurt to let them know I was in need of a car but didn't have a lot of money. That very same day I received a phone call from one of them saying that his friend had a car for sale and all he wanted was $100. What kind of car am I getting for only one hundred bucks? I thought. But then the Lord quickly reminded me that it was what He had provided. So I rejoiced. That afternoon we met to make the transaction. When I first saw the car I was blown away, it was an old blue station wagon, a Chrysler in fact. I was concerned that it may not even make it out of the parking lot. But the owner assured me that it was in good running condition and that I could count on it to get me from point A to point B. He let me know that the car had one of the best engines that Chrysler had ever built, a slant six. I asked, "What's a slant six?" He replied, "It has six cylinders and will run as long as you keep her oil changed right." Trying to appear business savvy about the car I asked, "What about the wires and spark plugs?" He replied, "They are all good." I gave him the money and rejoiced in what the Lord had told me. When I went down to the DMV to register and pay taxes I realized just how much I had to rejoice about. The process was only $35, which was indeed a blessing. As the previous owner had promised, the car worked just fine.

I was able to continue my school obligations and attended as far away as Natchez Mississippi, which was over 180 miles away. I went every weekend, which led all the way up to my first level of ordination in the AME

Church. This was a really big event for me and being ready to take my finals along with my other class members was even more critical. The old blue station wagon was averaging about 400 plus miles a week and purring like a kitten. Yes, the Lord had provided and I was rejoicing all the way.

Chapter 18:
Family Telephone "Ring" Conference

After our encounter with God's blessings at the Alabama bus station, Jacqui and I continued to talk on the phone. Jacqui agreed to discuss the possibility of marriage. Of course I had to meet her mother and perhaps a few other important people in her life. At Jacqui's insistence I had telephone conversations with three of her previous pastors, who also asked me questions and verified my faith in God. To my relief they gave Jacqui an approval to continue talking with me. I did not understand why I had to talk to all of these different people. I felt that it was clear that God wanted us to be together. But I went along since it was very important to her.

We had become accustomed to spending hours on the phone planning as we forged ahead looking on with excitement at the coming day of our marriage. We had set a tentative date just between the two of us, for the end of May Memorial Day weekend. Jacqui said if she was going to get married she wanted it to be in the spring. Now I must confess, at that time I wasn't the best when it came to long drawn-out planning sessions. As for me, most of my life had been pretty much spontaneous. With this lady I soon came to understand that I needed to get on the ball, realizing that I still needed to get a ring for the engagement as well as the wedding bands. I knew that if I was to demonstrate my ability to lead, I had to be proactive and master the habit.

One afternoon I received a call from Jacqui. She had arranged an impromptu phone call that included her mother on the other end of the line. Her voice was lively and filled with the joy of the Lord. She had a kind of warmness that seemed to bridge the distance between us. After chatting awhile, I wanted to get right down to the business at hand. After all the formalities I took a deep breath and said to her, "I would very much like to have your daughters hand in marriage." After talking a bit she said that we had her blessing and that she wanted to do something special for us. I can't tell you what a sigh of relief I experienced with hearing her approval that day! She proceeded to tell us that she wanted to give us the engagement rings from her marriage to Jacqui's father who had passed on. I paused for a moment thinking of the very small ring that that I had put on layaway from the pawnshop and quickly replied, "I would be honored to have it." We set up a time a time for her mother and I to travel to South Carolina to formally meet. I was to get the ring and resize it before our wedding. We finally agreed to set the date for the middle of March. It became very clear to me that Jacqui was not a person to mess around with when it came to following through with plans. Well before you could say one, two, three, she had already made the reservation and was calling to let me know how to pick up the flight ticket.

As usual time passed quickly and the day was finally upon us. I needed to have someone drop me off at the Gulfport Regional Airport. So who else could I call on beside my best men, Trent and Eric? I told them both about the trip and that I would need someone to get me to the airport. On that evening I needed to work late to finish up a project for the base. I was getting a bit worried about making my flight so Trent and Eric pitched in and helped me out. We were just finishing up when Eric asked me what time my flight was for that evening. I let him know my flight was due to leave at 5:30 p.m. He then made me aware that it was fifteen minutes after. I dropped everything and sped out the door. By the time we made it to the airport I found out that I had indeed missed my flight. We found out the flight was on its way to New Orleans and that there was a thirty minute layover to take on more passengers. We asked the ticket clerk to arrange for me to board in New Orleans. We dashed out to the car and Eric left the lot doing sixty mph, and before you could count to ten we were on the interstate doing at least 140 mph and arriving at the air terminal with five minutes to spare. It was a miracle that we didn't get a speeding ticket or get involved in a car accident.

As I landed in Greenville S.C., Jacqui and her Mother met me at the airport. I had not taken the time to think very much about what I would say when introduced to her mother. I must confess, I was a bit nervous about meeting her and the nearly missed flight. What were her expectations? Would I measure up? These are just some of the questions that ran through my mind. When the time came I did the first thing that came to mind, I reached out to hug her, and she welcomed me. The conversation between us flowed like old friends as we shared our confidence in the Lord. This meeting confirmed the statement, you will never meet a stranger in the Lord.

Jacqui's mother wanted to get right down to the business of getting the ring to me. I suppose that took a great deal of trust to be willing to release something so precious to someone she was introduced over the phone and had personally met only moments earlier. I believed she trusted me and of a certainty I wasn't going to betray that kind of trust.

Just moments later Mrs. Thompson took out a ring that was adorned with seven diamonds. One looked as though it was a one-carat by itself, the whole lot had to be at least two carats. I could hardly believe I was to be the guardian of this prize. I thanked her for the confidence she had in me to wed her daughter.

After that Jacqui took me to a local mall. There, we found a jeweler that we felt confident would do a good job at designing a setting for the diamond that we were just blessed with. He brought out several setting designs but we elected to design one of our own. After about an hour of drawing and sketching, we were pleased with a very unique and beautiful wedding set. The price came to be $450 with taxes. I put $50 down and we agreed that I would pay the remaining amount when I returned at the end of April. I had to leave to return to Biloxi the next day. It was my responsibility to preach at Sunday service when the pastor was out of town. To ensure that I would be there on Sunday I returned to town on Saturday. As quickly as the adventure started, it had come to an end, and I was back in Biloxi.

Jacqui's job and wedding planning consumed much of her time. She would occasionally contact me with instruction regarding what my role was to be in the wedding ceremony. I once asked her about what was going on in her life during that time. Her reply was everything you can imagine. There was the matter of applying for the marriage license. We then had the matter of catering the food and the setting up the wedding chapel. Somehow it all was going to work out. It wasn't until after our wedding that I found out that we had a family team that was ready to do anything that they could to help Jacqui have a beautiful wedding day. The entire affair and activities were planned around my preparation for ordination into the Deaconate Order of Ministry. I was working fulltime in the Air Force and attending classes along with the various quarterly meeting requirements. It was all like a whirlwind and all passed by in a flash

Chapter 19:
A Lesson In Increasing Faith

What I'm about to share with you has very little to do with Jacqui and I coming together but I thought it to be a wonderful faith-building testimony, one that demonstrates God's goodness and the faith of a saint that I was counted worthy to experience.

For certain my days passed by as a child's night before a seemingly distant Christmas morning. Every moment was laden with almost an ethereal anticipation of the day Jacqui and I chosen to wed. Of course there were the tasks of my daily duties as a Non Commissioned Officer in the United States Air Force, and at times it was extremely taxing. On one afternoon, while finishing up at work, a small voice pressed into my conscious world and whispered into my ear, "Go home to your mother now." I had never felt such a strong urge. As a matter of fact I thought I was losing it and should tell someone. It was such a strong and persistent voice and after much internal debate I followed the instruction. I packed my belongings. It was really strange pulling together clothes for that weekend and feeling a pressing for me to do it. As I made the 140-mile trip that I had taken several times before, I had a feeling that something was out of sorts this time. My mind soon became distracted with thoughts of Jacqui. Her return to South Carolina was filled with a long night on the phone sharing her recent experiences with her mother and family. She was very excited about how God used her as an instrument of deliverance and was glad to have her sisters and mother hear her story. While I was engrossed in the hopes of my future, that foreboding feeling suddenly returned. This time I felt like something terrible was about to happen. I began to pray and somehow my spiritual eyes were being opened to the potential gravity of this trial. I took a quick assessment of what was going on. I had this chilling sensation. I looked around and did not see anything. Suddenly, out of the blue I saw what appeared to be this strange creature on the hood of my car. It faded in and out of view. I could see it, then I couldn't. Then it was as if time slowed down. The image played over and over in my mind. Then something took over, my inner man had registered. I suddenly cried with a loud voice, "In the name of Jesus, I bind you!" Interrupted by a loud noise, I looked in to the rearview mirror. There was a big thump under the car and I could see what looked like tire tread flying down the road. I was still tooling down the road between sixty and sixty-five miles per hour; I hadn't swerved or lost control. I then regained my composure as best I could and pulled off the road. Getting out of the car quickly, I walked around the passenger side to assess any damage. As I walked around the car I noticed that all of the tread and tire wall on the right front tire were completely gone. I soon realized that I had been driving on inner wall and tub and did not experience a blow out. I stopped and pondered for a moment. I should have had a blow out and lost control but I believed an angel of the Lord bore me up. This was something like a miracle out of the Bible! I know this may sound kind of hokey, but it happened and that wasn't all. I didn't have a spare tire, so I had to drive another ten miles to Gautier, Mississippi. Creeping along at about five or six miles per hour, it took until 11:30 p.m. to find a tire shop. I was barely able to convince one of the clerks to help me out. I purchased two used tires that the clerk wasn't supposed to sell, but it was truly all I could afford. With my restored car and having gone through what I called interesting to say the least, I was even more determined to get home to see Chief. As the night was turning into early morning I arrived home and crept in and fell fast asleep.

Early the next morning the whispering voice started up again, this time instructing me to get up and go to the store. Now, I had only laid down a few hours earlier, but driven, I got up and went out on the task as instructed. By the time I was ready to check out I had a basket filled with groceries and really wasn't quite sure how I was going to pay for it. I had a debit card and I had only used it once. I decided to use it as instructed and don't you know the debit cleared $98 in groceries! There turned out to be an early payday for the military and it couldn't have come at a better time. Thank God! I hurried on home to get the groceries to Chief, still wondering if my shopping was the reason for the trip. As I walked in with the bags of food she said, "I sure didn't know where our next meal was going to come from; I was boiling some salt pork and cooking this last little rice." She let me know that folks had really been nice to her about it, but hated to keep begging them for stuff. As I listened to her speak, my eyes began to well up with tears, but I couldn't let her see me break down. So, I held them back and began to unpack the bags and put the food away. I couldn't help thinking she was doing everything a mother could do to help her son with his child and God heard those prayers. It became clear that it was the Spirit of the Lord whispering in my ear. He moved me to come here and that strange creature was a demon trying to hinder me from reaching her. This was an attempt to prevent the seeds of faith from growing in my mother. But He who had begun a great work in her was faithful to complete it.

Chapter 20:
Favor

After my whirlwind visit, I returned to work and tried to stay focused on my daily duties. I had been at work with my hands full working on sand blasting and polishing several crowns. It was around ten o'clock on the Wednesday morning of that week, when I finished up and decided to check my phone messages. Apparently sometime during my sand blasting, I received a call from the payroll office for the Air Force. I can remember the unnerving feeling that came over me as I listened to the message. I thought to myself as I listened, I have heard about these people, they don't have any mercy. Over the years I had heard tales about the people in that office and believe me, none of the dealings with them ended with a "happily ever after." They were cold as ice, as far as I knew. After musing a bit I got up enough nerve to call them back. The woman on the other end of the phone was very professional but very to the point. She let me know that I would need to report to their office. When I arrived she asked me to explain why I had stopped the child support allotment. I explained, "Let me start by saying, almost ten months ago I was placed under court order to pay child support and alimony for Carol and DeWayne Junior in the amount of $350 per month. I stopped payment when I found the child abandoned about three months earlier." I further explained to her that my son was currently living with my mother and that I was the only one providing support for the child and dealing with the tens of thousands in bills that my former wife was responsible for. The payment officer looked at me and said she really wasn't sure why she was doing what she was about to do. She then picked up her phone and dialed a number. I heard her ask to speak to my squadron commander and was relieved when I remembered that he and I had an excellent working relationship. I was not sure how he would respond regarding the mess that I had found myself in this time, so I sat down and decided to pray and listen intently to every word she spoke as she began to tell him that she had me in her office. She recounted what I had shared with her earlier and asked my commander if it was credible. At that moment I really wasn't sure how he would respond. Again, I really had not spoken with him regarding the matter since he had helped me get into the dorms the previous year. However, his response was, "Whatever Sergeant Thomas said you can believe it to be true." She said that she had never gotten a response like that before and that she would normally require a signature from a commander to do a stop order on a wage garnishment of more than $1,500. She then said that I did not need to worry about it anymore. This was the first event releasing me of the money ties to my ex-wife! This was a great victory for me as I was no longer obligated to pay child support or alimony. I rejoiced because I could now work on the outstanding bills and restoring my credit. Once again the God of my salvation had shown Himself strong. It was becoming more and more evident to me that if I trusted in God and kept my faith He would never fail me. The constant recurrences of God's favor in my life moved me to a greater faith, the type of faith that would be needed for the future challenges, which were yet to be revealed.

Chapter 21:
More Than What's Asked

Before I realized it, the time had come for me to return to pay for the rings. I arrived in the city of Spartanburg just outside of Greenville, South Carolina. I arrived a bit early because I was still a little antsy about the money needed to purchase all that was required of me. It had only been a few days after my reprieve from paying child support. I went straight to the mall where the jeweler was located. I produced my receipt and gave the cashier my name and an attendant came over and let me know that it would be a few minutes wait as they were in the process of polishing the set. She then proceeded to say, "In the meantime while you wait, here is your receipt, it has been paid in full." I was sure after hearing her say this that they had the wrong receipt. After close examination of the ticket I saw that it had my name on it and my signature from when I dropped off the diamonds. I asked if they knew who had been to the shop to make the payment. They called the master jeweler who confirmed that the ticket was correct and said I should not worry about it. After getting over the shock and the pleasant surprise of being relieved of the remaining $400 that was due, I could only thank God for his goodness! When they brought the set out I was amazed at the beauty of the setting itself, the jeweler had done a wonderful job. I figured that Jacqui had somehow come into some extra money to pay off the rings. Either way, I knew that I would need to help her in any way that I could. More than satisfied, I left he jeweler and moved to the next big thing on my agenda—arranging the proper location for my formal proposal and presentation of the rings!

Chapter 22:
The Big Dinner

After leaving the jewelers I was on cloud nine. The unexplained payment and the marvelous work that was done on the rings added to the excitement of my proposal plan. As I drove along the main drag, I saw a beautiful Chinese restaurant, the Green Dragon Garden. I thought of the first formal date we had shared and how it had been at a similar eatery. I decide to stop and check it out. It was nice inside and had a great menu, and off to the side was a beautiful rock and oriental ornament garden. There was a wonderful footpath that led to a lit seating area. I decided right then, that this is where I will present the rings to her. I made the reservation for us and since I was pressed for time I had to return to Biloxi that same night. For this trip I had rented a car and driven to see her.

I left the restaurant and went directly to her place. When I arrived she was expecting me and met me at the door. She had plans to take me around to see a few pastors but when we arrived at the church they were not available. We decided to have some lunch at a pizza eatery and spend the day visiting her friends and few of her family members. The day was moving on so I thought I had better let her know what my plans were for the evening. I said to her, "I have something special I would like to share with you." She was really excited about my little announcement and was pleased to return to her apartment to get dressed. As I waited for her to get ready, I decided to take a short nap and when I awoke I saw her looking as beautiful as ever. We went to the restaurant and attempted to eat dinner but due to the nerves of anticipation, we both ate very little.

It was finally time for my proposal as I led her out to the place past the beautiful stone carving and lanterns. She looked radiant as her eyes glistened in the soft light from the lanterns. We made our way to the sitting area, and there surrounded by beauty and the sweet smell of jasmine flowers, I kneeled down on one knee. I opened the box to present the rings and asked her if she would be my wife. She expressed her joy with smiles and tears and a sweet, "Yes." Wow, it had come true, I had really asked her to marry me and she had responded with yes! The exuberant feeling could not be contained or explained, the love of my life would soon be my bride. Now, there was the matter of expressing my appreciation for her for paying the rings off. As I attempted to express my deepest gratitude, she surprised me by letting me know that she had not paid anything on the rings and that she was barely able to keep up the payment on her credit card and their very large phone bill. I began to share with her what happened moments earlier at the jewelers. She made a few phone calls later that evening to find out if the only two other people who know about the rings had paid them off. They both denied making the payment. The only explanation that we could come up with was that it was the Lord. He had made it happen by supernatural means and we realized that once again God had stepped into our lives and worked another miracle.

Chapter 23:
The Holy Ghost Hook up

My next visit to Greenville was to help Jacqui pack up her apartment. As usual, when you have a tight budget you begin, what I like to call, "the box scavenge." So we went to different stores trying to locate and collect boxes. After scurrying about town looking for boxes we found ourselves back at the apartment. I will never forget what would happen that evening. As I was assisting her with wrapping up her crystal to be placed in the boxes, the Television was on. A TV special captured my attention. R.W. Schambach, a great evangelist, was airing a camp meeting. I knew about him because Jacqui had introduced me to his ministry several years earlier. Now, I had no idea that Jacqui had been floored by the simple fact that R.W. Schambach was on TV and, on top of it all he was preaching on the Baptism of the Holy Ghost! He began to explain the necessity of the baptism of Holy Ghost to do the works of Jesus Christ. I sat there watching with my eyes and ears glued to every word that fell from his lips. Unbeknownst to me Jacqui was listening as well and started to quietly whisper in prayer. The evangelist explained how the Holy Ghost worked through us and provided dunamos, power without end. When I heard him say this I said to myself, I want that. I turned around and said to Jacqui, "I want that." She replied, "We can pray right now." She prayed for me to receive as I asked God to baptize me in the Holy Ghost with evidence of other tongues. Before I could even think about what it would be like, I was speaking in other tongues and praying in the spirit. I was so excited that I ran through the house leaping and jumping. Jacqui said, "You have Him!" I shouted, "I know!" She then let me know that I needed to practice praying in the Spirit often. After things calmed down somewhat, Jacqui said to me, "I think it's time to share something with you, something that I haven't shared with anyone." I really couldn't imagine what it was that she wanted to share with me before anyone else. What secret could this be? As she took me by the hand and lead me into her kitchen she told me to have a seat. As I sat at the kitchen table she stepped away for a moment to the refrigerator reaching over to its hidden side, she said, "Here it is." As she pulled a semi folded piece of paper off the side of her refrigerator, she placed the paper on the table in front of me and told me to read it. Looking down at it, at first glance it appeared to be a shopping or grocery list. But after I read the heading I saw that it said, "Lord, if he is the one, here is the list of things that must happen for me to marry him." There were seven things on the list:

1. He needs to be accepted and blessed by my mother.
2. He needs to be blessed by my pastors.
3. He needs to be free from alimony.
4. He needs to have no legal or financial issues.
5. He needs to be baptized in the Holy Ghost speaking in other tongues.
6. He needs to be free from financial ties to ex-wife with no joint property.
7. He needs to have complete custody of his son.

As I sat at the table looking down I could see that all but two of the item had been lined through. She took the pen in her hand and reaching over me she crossed through the item listed fifth on the list. God had been eliminating items from the list she had written. Then she asked, "Do you remember all of the pastors I insisted that you meet? If they had told me no, then we would not be planning a wedding right now. If my mother had said no, then we would have had to stop everything. If you had not been released from the thirty thousand dollar bad check charge it would have all stopped. If God didn't free you of the wage garnishment for child support and alimony, well, it would have stopped things." The faith that it must have taken her to surrender completely to God was astounding. I was overcome with joy as I thought back to the many times I was completely dependent on God to deliver me from the overwhelming situations. I reached across the table and held her hand as we began to pray a prayer of thanksgiving to the God of our salvation. We acknowledged that it was but by Your hand that we had been brought together and for certainty we believed we have your blessing. It had been the best thing when Jacqui had insisted that we walk away from each other. It was the only way that this relationship could be pure and holy. After which we danced around the apartment praising the living God! That night I spent time practicing the prayer language that the Holy Spirit had given me. The next day I realized that I could open my mouth and choose to speak in my new prayer language. I could engage the Holy Spirit anytime I wanted! No, I was not possessed. I had a helper and a comforter. It was a true blessing, another precious gift the Lord had given me.

Chapter 24:
The Heavenly Hook Up

I pondered what had happened over the last few days as I left town to return to Biloxi. When I arrived, I called to let Jacqui know that I had a check for the tux rental and could now pay for the best man and grooms' tuxedoes as well. We agreed that I would also pay for the wedding flowers. Thank God for the back pay from the held wages! Jacqui in the meantime was still very busy working on the plans for her wedding dress. In addition to preparing for the wedding as well, I continued my toil up and down the highways attending classes and meetings to ensure I had met all of the mandatory requirements to be admitted into the Eighth District of the AME Church. When I tell you it was a difficult road, I mean difficult. The classes and some of the assignments seemed to never end. In addition to that, my pastor had made me the point man for what we called, "The Hour of Power." It was program that happened once a month that involved singing and prayer with words of exhortation. It started out small but soon became very popular among the local church folk. Our lives were really full at this point and before we realized it, there were only a few days before the big day!

As time dwindled down I decided to take time off to go to Birmingham to tend to some of the final details. When I arrived I was introduced to Jacqui's side of the family who resided there. They welcomed me with open arms and I couldn't help but feel right at home. They treated me just like one of the family. I was picked on and protected. I was fed and laughed at, imagine that, and with total disregard of my newness to the brood. All of the details for the wedding where coming together nicely and soon it was time to find a wedding band for me. Seeing as how we were pretty low on cash, I suggested that we look for a pawnshop for a band. Now, Jacqui really didn't want to have anything to do with a pawnshop and thought we should try looking in a few jewelry stores. So we spent the entire day looking in stores trying to find a band that was heavy enough and large enough for my finger. Finally I told her, "Sweetheart let's face it, we don't have the money to do it this way." With that being said, I finally convinced her to look in the pawnshops. Facing the reality of this, she cried before we went inside to take a look around. But we were able to find a large gold wedding band for $78. It would need to be resized but they guaranteed that it would be ready the next day. Everything was now in place except for the wedding rehearsal.

Later that night we were to have the rehearsal and I should let you know that I had completely forgotten to tell the groomsman and my best man the time and location of the wedding and that they needed to show up for the rehearsal. The pastor was there and after about thirty minutes of nail biting and waiting, I had to tell my pastor about my oversight. Pastor Patterson wanted to demonstrate his support and blessing on my marriage. He drove all the way from Biloxi just for the ceremony and had to leave immediately to return to church on Sunday morning. When I told him of my oversight, He just smiled and told me, "It's going to be alright." Minutes later, the little Toyota MR 2 pulled into the parking lot and out jumped Eric and Trent. When they came in, I ran to greet them and Eric with his cool demeanor said, "It's good that B'ham is my old stomping grounds, cause bro you left us hanging." I started to apologize to him for forgetting and before I could attempt to further explain, he interrupted me, pointing to Catherine, the Maid of Honor, and said, "Not a problem, just introduce me to her." I was surprised at his response, yet relieved that he wasn't angry and told him, "Sure." So, we made it through the rehearsal and the dinner smoothly and soon I was back at the hotel glad for a moment of solitude and rest.

Morning seemed to come so quickly the next day. I can recall standing in front of the mirror in the bathroom almost in a trance and saying aloud, "Lord, this is the right thing; I want this to be for a lifetime. Today, you are going to marry the prize of your life. Today, Jacqui Thompson will become Jacqui Thomas. I will see the promise of the Lord come to pass this day in my life." Before I slipped on my white tux, I kneeled and thanked the Lord for all he had done for Jacqui and I. I remember praying a prayer along these lines, "Dear Lord more than a year ago I was seemingly at the bottom of the world. I was sitting in a home that had been stripped down and was as empty as a cave. Everything was taken from me. I was brought down and made low, but my God you did not forsake me. When I came to myself, and called upon you, Father you heard from Heaven and answered my cry and in the midst of my sorrow and you rescued me and in your mercy you promised to return my son to me. Father you did that. Then, you promised to give me my wife, Father you have done that. Now, Oh Father I believe you for the restoration of my home seven times greater than before. Thank you, Father. Thank you. Amen, Amen, and Amen." After praying a bit, I finished getting dressed and not long after that, a knock came at the door. It was Johnnie, Jacqui's eldest sister; she had arrived to pick me up for the wedding. I grabbed my bag and I jumped in the car. This was my first time meeting her sister and she offered kind words of encouragement as we drove along. As we rode along I found it difficult to concentrate. My mind was rambling with thoughts of hope, joy and love. I was waiting in anticipation of the so-called "cold feet" but they never showed up. I guess I forgot to send them an invite. As we traveled, it felt as though we had been driving for only a few minutes and we had arrived at the chapel. Our guests seemed to all be arriving. We had given only a few invitations and almost everyone invited was there. My mother, Chief, along with DJ and the rest of the family were all there with smiles. It was good to see so many show up, as it is quite a drive from Century, Florida to Birmingham, Alabama Jacqui's family, specifically Mrs. Thompson along with Aunty Betty, Jean, Marquita and Juanita had the place looking splendid. Jacqui had insisted on peach and green as being the accent colors for our nuptials. I must confess I was a bit opposed to it at first but it became more palatable as our big day drew closer. Jacqui and her Maid of Honor, Catherine, were in the back room putting on the finishing touches.

They were fussing so much about the little things that when the music for the brides march came around, they missed it and forgot to give my beautiful bride her bouquet. Although this was missing, the radiance from her smile filled its place. Her beauty filled the room and captured everyone around her. I stood there as she made her way toward the alter and what was to be our ceremony. Her father pro tem, Pastor Roscoe, gave her away. I thought about the words of wisdom he had given us and of course his blessing on the marriage, which played a huge part towards the fruition of the day.

The pastor moved us through the ceremony with ease and my heart raced with excitement. In my mind, I was saying, Can we get to the end? But my spirit was relishing every moment of the way. Then the time came when we were to repeat our vows, as we looked into each other eyes I had a perfect peace. We placed the rings on each other's fingers. We then had Holy Communion after which we were presented to the public for the first time as Mr. and Mrs. DeWayne M. Thomas, husband and wife.

I can remember standing for the pictures as the praise and worship team began singing. Jacqui's sister, Johnnie, began to speak great things over our marriage as we entered the hall for our wedding celebration. The people were all smiles and the room was filled with delight and laughter. We did not take anyone's presence lightly, for just being there to celebrate with us was a great honor. Most of them had traveled many miles to be there. So many of them came and presented wonderful gifts to us, which were indeed a bonus to the momentous occasion. I can remember the admonishments from Jacqui's sisters to take care of their baby sister. A funny thing too, I was getting the same admonishments from my folks. I guess it was plain to see that I was getting the best part of the deal. In the back of my mind I made a promise to never forget that I had been given the prize. You should know that Mrs. Thompson didn't spare too much change in the post wedding celebration. It was quite an affair to share in and remember for all time. As we were about to leave the hall, we saw a beautiful limo adorned in full wedding regalia and a driver awaiting us in front of the hall. After we departed we were driven throughout the city with signs announcing our marriage; it was quite the spectacle. I was not sure where we were headed until we arrived at the Hilton. As we disembarked for our room, everything had been taken care of. Needless to say our first night as husband and wife was wonderful.

The following morning we would be on our way to our honeymoon in Pensacola, Florida. It was only a day or two, but we had such a wonderful time driving around town, looking at the old historic district, Rosy O-Grady's and all the other sites. It was a walk down memory lane for me. I had always wanted to share it with someone special. We enjoyed the shore and the beautiful surf as it rolled in on the snow-white sandy beaches. We enjoyed the sand as it squeezed up between our toes during our wonderful conversation. Even though we wanted to spend forever basking in the moment, time was short and money was even shorter. We wanted to stay but we had to return to our lives and get settled into our future together.

Chapter 25:
Little Cabin for My Lady

Now before I left town to get married, I spoke with one of the members of my church in Biloxi, about renting her mother-in-law's suite for a month or two until we were able to get an apartment. Please understand that I hadn't taken the time to check out the apartment before I agreed to enter in a contract. She was a member from our church. I had been to her home on several occasions and it was truly lavish. Her house had been filled with wonderful finery and amenities so much so I just believed that for $200 I would be getting a nice little start for us in the in-law suite. As we arrived at our landlord's home, Jacqui was just amazed as I was at the splendor of her house. I could see the excitement in her eyes; Jacqui had naturally assumed as well that the suite would be of the same décor.

To our surprise and my embarrassment it was not so. Now, the landlord had not promised me splendor, I just assumed splendor. The little cottage was clean but very small. It consisted of a single small room and a bathroom. In fact, it was so small we could lie in the bed and flip a pancake on the stove. The bathroom was a very small partition with a sink, commode and a shower stall. We almost had to step outside to change clothes. I looked at my new bride knowing that this was a far cry from her previous living conditions; I reassured her that everything would be fine and it would all work out. Although my reassurance to her was firm, I was thinking the whole while that this could not possibly be our apartment until we left for Guam.

Chapter 26:
Angel Along the Way

We didn't have much time to complain about anything. I was preparing for the big annual conference for the AME Church. During this time they examined licentiates hoping to be ordained into the Deaconate Order. Time was short and the schedule was tight and we needed to make our way there quickly. As we began to get acquainted again, Jacqui shared with me that she was amazed with God's humor. Marrying a minister was one of the things she was pretty determined she would not do, but here she was married to one and on her way with him to be ordained. She had not understood that in the AME Church ordination into the Deaconate was the same as being ordained as a minister. She thought it was training to become a Deacon. This time the laugh was definitely on her.

Thankfully, we had some of the monies given to us as wedding gifts, and Jacqui's newly purchased car was in good condition. I would say by God's grace, we were in great shape. Now, all we needed was to go to Century and get DJ. We decided to have him with us during the annual conference.

Well, after much prayer and preparation we were off. I can recall us praying as we left town for Natchez, Mississippi. We loosed our angels and as we were rolling along in the car, suddenly I saw out of the corner of my right eye what appeared to be an angelic being. I was startled at first until I realized what it was. Now, as I turned to get a better look, I could see this being with skin that resembled white mother of pearl. His hair was white and he was dressed in all white apparel. And there was light around him. My heart raced with excitement at the reality of seeing an actual angel. If that wasn't enough, the being turned and looked back inside the car and smiled at me. During the whole while he did not speak a word to us. All of this took place while traveling down the road at about sixty mph. I can remember those piercing eyes looking back into our car and then calmly he turned his head away and with his hand he pointed forward. Then within a blink of an eye he went before us disappearing into the distance. I turn to Jacqui to ask if she witnessed what I'd just seen, to my disappointment she had not. She asked, "What did you see?" I said, "I saw what appeared to be an angel." She said, "Halleluiah! Our angels are going before us!" I was thankful that she had faith to believe that angels still walk among us. The Lord has said, "His angels encamp around those that put their trust in Him." Well bless God," I said. "He is a wonder all by Himself." And we then began to sing songs of Zion, psalms, hymns and spirituals as we traveled along the way. We didn't realize it at the time but we were building a tradition that continues until this day; when we travel we sing songs along the way. During this time we had one song that Jacqui played in particular called, "Jesus Can Work It Out." That was our shouting song. Jacqui played that song until she wore out the cassette. Well, I would like to share everything that took place while on this trip but time will not permit. However, I will say that after our little trip to the annual conference, the AME Church would never be the same.

Chapter 27:
What Ills Come This Way?

Shortly after conference, we started to settle into our new home. Jacqui had taken it upon herself to walk down to the grocery store to pick up some items to make a special dinner for yours truly, her husband. During what was to be just a simple little walk down the road turned into an ordeal that she would never forget. As she was returning from the store she felt a little faint. She thought it was just the Mississippi sun causing her to sweat profusely. She was not used to the humidity. I don't know if you've heard about the Mississippi humidity, but it can be so high that you can shower, dry off, clothe yourself in an air conditioned place, and by the time you make it to your air conditioned car, you will be dripping wet with sweat. But this had to be some-thing else, she thought. She was soon overtaken by her discomfort. Deciding to stop, she knocked on someone's door to ask for water. After drinking the water, her thirst was soon accompanied by dizziness and an extreme headache. Somehow, she made it back home to the cottage. When I arrived she had struggled to make the dinner and was awaiting me. I took one look at her and said that she should make an appointment to see a doctor. We called in to schedule her appointment. The following morning we arrived at the clinic and as we walked in they gave us both masks and said, "The doctor believes you may have chicken pox." They let us know there was no need to test based on her symptoms and that they would call in the medicine at the pharmacy. I said, "Well is the doctor sure? I had chicken pox when I was little." The tech replied, pointing us in the direction of the pharmacy, "I believe that he's sure." Well, we both were floored, though happily married for only a few weeks, there we were very miserable. The fever, the pain, and the itching were horrific. After being shut in the little cottage for two weeks, you can imagine the serious case of cabin fever we both had developed. We were ready to recharge our batteries and join the rest of the world.

Chapter 28:
A Restorative Hook Up

The chicken pox cleared up just in time for the court case for DeWayne Junior's change of custody petition. Our petition was presented before the Jefferson Family Court. I was concerned because I had difficulty just getting Carol to sign the divorce modification papers. Before she would sign, I had to agree to keep nothing. It was final; everything was hers' that she was willing to take payment responsibility for. We were completely financially untied. As the day drew closer, I felt I had good reason to be a bit concerned. I had gotten word from a friend regarding the disposition of the car that Carol received in the settlement. The car had been impounded and the note was behind. It wasn't a pretty picture by any means and I was interested to know how things would play out.

Well the day of the hearing was upon us. Jacqui and I had meticulously selected our attire to wear for this very import date. She was adorned in a snow-white summer dress and I chose to wear my grey pinstriped suit. We wanted to look acceptable and thought that our dress was a part of the evaluation. Our anticipation was building and tension was high. The whole thing was all about to come to a climax. I had been waiting for this day for quite some time and now all I wanted was for it to be over and done with. The torrent of emotion is an interesting feeling when you find yourself standing right at the edge of a great change in your life. You feel frightened, self-constrained, and courageous all at the same time. This strange cocktail of emotions can't just be summoned, yet somehow you will always find them present in times of great challenges. I can remember looking across our small bedroom and saying, "Well this is it, here we go." We made our way to the courthouse and to the family court.

As we walked in, I was surprised to find the room so crowded. We were obliged to take a seat in the rear of the room. The atmosphere was really intense. After waiting only a little while it felt as though we had been in the room forever. The lawyers were back and forth in litigation, trying to hammer out the final details of our presentation before the judge. Then my lawyer came to me and said that he had some not so great news. I asked him what the issue was and if he thought things would work out. He replied, "She is not moving on the custody issue. She wouldn't sign the papers and right now I really don't know what's going to happen." I looked over at Jacqui and could see that she was praying. I thought for a moment. Then the Word of the Lord came to me saying, "She will listen to you." I didn't hesitate. I quickly asked if I could go into the room where they been negotiating.

After being there for awhile and listening to them go back and forth, it was confirmed that they really weren't getting anywhere. I raised my hand and asked if I could talk to Carol alone and asked everyone to leave the room. Reluctantly, they all left. I was very prayerful as I looked over in her direction. In my mind I thought, If I say the wrong thing it could all be over, and the entire day would be a loss. She eventually lifted her head and looked into my eyes. I smiled, and she replied by nodding her head. I could see that she was in great anguish. Silently, I began to pray for her strength to do what was right for the child. I tried to think of words to demonstrate my empathy with her. I had no words. She was being asked to give up custody of her child. I felt by any standards that would be a hard pill to swallow for any mother. After she had given me a long piercing stare she broke the palpable silence. Solemnly whispering, "I have to give you little DeWayne Jr. now, don't I?" I softly replied, "Yes." Later, as I looked back at her response and remembered her using the word "now," it was as if she hoped it would be temporary, as though sometime in the future she would be back for him. You can't help noticing that the maternal instinct is a wondrous thing. For even after being greatly oppressed by the chains of chemicals, when freed it will cry out with its last breath. She hesitantly asked, "This is best for him now, right?" With great relief I replied, "Yes." As her eyes began to well with tears she leaned forward almost bowing in submission, her face less than an inch from the paper as she surrendered her signature. Doing this she was agreeing to surrender paramount custody and agreeing that it be conveyed to me. I called the lawyers back into the room and they took care of the rest of the paper work. At that point we all retired into the main courtroom. There we sat waiting our turn to be called before the magistrate.

After about an hour, I was summoned to the front of the courtroom. The clerk read the brief for everyone in the courtroom to hear. I can remember it starting out like, "Now comes before the Jefferson County Family Court, the matter of DeWayne M. Thomas Sr. vs. Carol Y. Monroe. Petition for modification of paramount custody of the..." There it was, read loud and clear for everyone present to hear whether they wanted to or not. Then after all of the reading, the magistrate took the papers and reviewed them and began to ask me questions. He started with, "Are you DeWayne M. Thomas Sr.?" I replied, "Yes, your honor, Sir." There was long pause. Then he said, "It's obvious that you are in the military. I understand that you have orders to travel to Guam, that's a long way from here." I said, "Yes your honor." He then asked how I proposed to take care of such a small child by myself. He went on to say, "I don't think you can do that alone in the military." I replied, "Your honor I'm no longer alone; as of May 27, 1989, I am married, Sir." I quickly beckoned to Jacqui to stand up. The court addressing her, asked if she was willing to assist me in the rearing of the child. She responded, "Yes, your honor." The magistrate took the paperwork and retired to his chambers to make his decision. We were then instructed to be seated and await his return. After a short while he returned. The bailiff announced the magistrate's return. "All rise and call the court into session." He seated us and I once again was summoned to the front. The magistrate announced, "I have decided to grant you paramount custody and visitation rights to Carol. She will be required to pay child support for the amount of $135. The child is the most important concern before us today." He admonished us to never forget to always do what is best for the child. With tears of joy, I took Jacqui into my arms and said, "If it had not been for you, I would not have been able to get my son."

The last item on her list was done. The hand of the law was supporting what God had already done months earlier. It was not in our time, but it was in God's time. We could barely wait to get home to tell Chief about the big decision regarding DJ. I just praised the Lord. He had promised me that He would restore my son back and give me my wife. Wow! Hallelujah! Hallelujah! Great is thy faithfulness, oh

Lord how excellent is they name! I shouted this over and over. Chief was just as jubilant as I was with her hands up in the air as she praised God. Well, I'm a living witness that if you just be patient and wait on the Lord, He will always keep His Word. I recalled the occasions when I was tempted to take matters into my own hands. I had once heard a minister say, "Only one man can drive the mule team at a time." And so it is with the reins of our lives with God. He is either Lord or He isn't. I took this lesson of truth to heart and prayed that God would help me to live by it.

Chapter 29:
God's Provisions

At this time we had a total of $600 to our name, which was given to us from the wedding. Now that we had full custody of DJ we definitely needed a larger living space. With this money we still needed a fully-furnished apartment which included a bedroom set, living room set, and groceries for all three of us. Well, when Jacqui came to me with her plan I must confess I was a bit unsure if we would be able to do all of it with what little money we had. I once asked Jacqui about what was going on in her mind at the time. She let me know that when I would speak about us not being able to do something, she simply reminded herself that she could do all things through Christ that strengthened her. I suppose she was thinking about the miracle of the fish and loaves. The irony of it all is that my lack of faith would be the catalyst that provoked her to hold on even tighter to her confession of faith. She had learned something that I had yet to fully understand. That lesson was that Christ is as big as you let him be in your faith and will do whatever you have faith to believe for. There is this scripture that goes kind of like this, "Take heed with what measure you believe, for the same measure shall be dealt unto you."

On this particular day she noticed an ad in the local paper for a king size bed with a chest of drawers and dresser. After reviewing the ad she decided she would speak with the owner. She got the directions to the place, and decided that we should drive out to take a look at the set. When we arrived we were completely surprised by what we found there. Wow! The set looked great but we thought that we would need to buy a mattress to make it work. Well guess what? The owner threw in the mattress for free. It was fairly new and all we needed to get was a slipcover. When the seller found out that we were just married she asked if we wanted the sheets and spread that went with it. We replied sure, and quickly expressed our thankfulness. We had just been blessed with an entire five-piece King sized bedroom set! Not to mention, she threw in a shoe rack to boot. What a blessing, and all for only $175.

Then, there was the matter of finding an apartment to put the stuff in. When Jacqui came to me with her plan to go and find an apartment and get us moved in with first and last months rent with only $300, I must confess I didn't believe she would be able to do it. But I learned enough about God and what he could do, so I agreed with her in faith and at the end of the day she called me to find out if I wanted to live on the beach, and if I could get someone to help move the bedroom set into the apartment. Jacqui had found an apartment for rent for only $225 and the landlord had agreed to waive the first month rent if we agreed to clean the apartment up before we moved in. I instantly agreed and let her know that I would have someone before the end of the day. Before the day was over, around three in the afternoon Jacqui called again to let me know that we now had a seven-piece living room set for only $150. The owner had agreed to let us pay two separate payments in addition to delivering it for us. All of these transactions occurred in two days time! It was a Wednesday when she made up her mind to do all of this and by the end of the day Thursday we had an apartment full of furniture, all for less than $600. I had been fully persuaded that with God all things are possible! "All things work together for the good of those who love the Lord and are called according to his purpose." There is nothing too small or too big for God.

We had moved into the apartment and at first I was a bit concerned that the furniture wouldn't fit in our small abode, but when it was all said and done everything fit perfectly. There we were Jacqui, little DJ, and I all nestled in our new home. But there was one slight problem and it kind of goes back to the reason we were able to get such a great deal on the move in. As I said earlier the landlord waived the first month rent if we agreed to take care of the move-in prep. Well, we cleaned the apartment top to bottom with degreaser and disinfectant. The place smelled great and looked clean however there was a problem. At night, after we turned the lights to go to bed, Jacqui decided to get up for that last cool drink of water. Just as she turned the light on she saw visitors. Yes, we had big and little visitors called cockroaches! Now, if that was not bad enough my wife started to scream and yell for me to come and kill them. She absolutely hated them and demanded that I do something. While I wanted to demonstrate my absence of fear, I was dead beat tired. I replied, "Don't worry, baby, I will take care of them in the morning. I will pick up some spray tomorrow. Just come back to bed before you wake DJ." She then started going on and on about what if they bother DJ while he's sleeping. Finally, when she saw that I wasn't going to get up to try and kill what was probably hundreds of those boogers, she said, "Lets pray that God will kill them." I said, "Dear, don't waste God's time doing stuff that we can take care of. Besides, God doesn't have time for stuff like that anyway." She replied clearly frustrated, "I'm going to pray to my Father and he will answer my prayer even for this." Well, what was I to do? I wasn't going to argue about the finer points about whether God would be an ever-present help in a time of need concerning roaches. No, I wasn't going to do it. So, I lay down and covered my head and she did as well, but not without a prayer. This is some of what she prayed, "Father, I thank you for your hedge of protection around me. Father we paid our tithes, and with that you promised that you would rebuke the devourer. You said, no pestilence shall come nigh unto us. Father I loose my angels to go forth and minister in our behalf." After hearing her prayer, I softly agreed with her hoping that would be enough to allow me to get some shuteye.

At about 5:00 the next morning, I got up as I normally would to use the bathroom. I stepped out of the bed and walked to the bathroom half asleep. I really wasn't paying much attention to what was happening around me. As I slowly started to glance around I saw dead and dying roaches all around me. I could not believe my eyes! Jacqui's prayer had worked and I dashed into the bedroom being careful not to crush any more. I crawled into bed and shook Jacqui awake. I half shouted, "They are dead and dying all around us!" Still half asleep, she asked, "What are you talking about?" I said excitedly, "The roaches are dead! The roaches are dead!" And she rolled over and calmly said, "We prayed didn't we?" My response was kind of silly but very sincere, "God does answer even the prayer for the extermination of the insects." Then I thought, Well, He can command the insects. He demonstrated that with one of the plagues against Egypt. Anyway, God had dispatched an angel to deal with our roach problem. Later that morning, I got up and swept up two dustpans full of roaches I tell you we had no more roaches after that.

Now, you may remember that I previously shared that Carol took my car when she initially left taking everyone and everything. Well, I received a notice from the courthouse that the car had been impounded after Carol had been arrested for a number of unfortunate things. When I heard about this, I went down to pick up the car and was able to turn it in. Turning it in freed me from the outstanding debt which was about $15,000 that still remained on the loan. The goodness of God truly knew no end and kept showing up time after time.

I can recall one morning, as we were preparing to pack for Guam, my new wife asked what was for breakfast. I had been in the kitchen and knew that there wasn't any real food, so I prayed. God answered my prayers and instructed me make some biscuits with only mayonnaise, flour and water. We didn't have syrup so I made some from scratch using butter and brown sugar. Everything turned out great and I could see that my family was happy and thankful. Later that day a friend came by with a large bag of groceries and said that the Lord told his wife to send it over.

These events were just a few of the many things and miracles that God worked out on our behalf. One thing we had learned for certain was that God would be as involved in our lives as we let Him be. The stories are great and the ways are many that have been wrought by the hand of God in our lives. But those are stories for another time.

About the Author

My Name is DeWayne M. Thomas and by the grace of God I have been afforded the opportunity to live out my dreams. I'm the husband to Jacqui, my wife of several wonderful years and a father of two sons, both of which I'm well pleased with. During the past twenty-four years I became an ordained elder and pastor. My wife and I are both family-life educators. We have established R.E.L.A.T.E., Inc., a nonprofit corporation dedicated to restoring the foundations for healthy relationships. As presenters we are certified in Prevention Relationship Enhancement Program (PREP), 7 Habits of Highly Effective Family, as well as Active Relationship by Kelly Simpson, MBTI, and several other trainings to enable us to accomplish our vision. God has even allowed us to design several trainings that we have shared with organizations and churches. We have presented various relationship education and life skills coursed to hundreds of individuals around the world. I am most thankful for having the opportunity to share and relive some of God's blessings in my life.

HOW TO HAVE A HEAVENLY HOOK UP:
A supplemental study guide

By Jacqui Thomas

Preface

As a young Christian, I received lots of advice concerning work ethic, doing what is right and demonstrating Christian love. When it came down to matters concerning relationships with the opposite sex, I was usually left to figure it out. I thought mutual physical attraction sufficed as a definition for equally yoked and I ended up making some really poor decisions. Don't get me wrong, the people of God always had something to say about relationships, but it wasn't specific enough. Recommendations like, "Mind you manners," and "Don't bite off more than you can chew," did not exactly provide the guidance needed for finding a wife. My wife, Jacqui's guidance on preparing for a mate was definitely more specific than mine. As a child, she was not brought up in the church. As a matter fact she was taught not to play church. Her understanding was that you should not go until you are ready to be real with God. So it wasn't until she was around sixteen years old that she found herself seeking to know who this God was. The good thing about all this is, when she found God, it was real. To help her with all this was the Baptism of the Holy Ghost and an old soldier who had not yet compromised, but yet was living Holy. Because of this truth I have asked my wife, Jacqui, to present to your thirsty minds a "How To" supplement guide. This is her work. I pray that you are blessed by it.

Preparing for a Heavenly Hook Up

Why is this topic important? God is very interested in our relationships. However, being the gentleman that He is, He waits for a sincere and true invitation to be intricately involved in our affairs. Often, we wonder how is it that we seem to continue to end up in the wrong types of relationships. The answer is that when it comes to relationships, God does not agree to be a co-pilot. He must be the pilot in order to chart the course and navigate any necessary course corrections because He is the only who actually knows the destination. Since, in our society we grow up with a fundamental belief that we are the rulers of our destiny, the idea of completely yielding to an intangible, invisible God is almost incomprehensible.

In this workbook, I will present some fundamental actions and attitudes necessary to yield the piloting of your relationships to God. I also want to say that as was demonstrated the testimony of our courtship, we need God's intervention in all of relationships. Not just marital, but also in community, financial, work related, social and familial connections.

As I was praying about how to communicate the insight that God has shared with me on this matter, God has given me six life standards for marital preparation, in the form of an acronym, that I will use to specify how to make God central in our relationships and to allow Him to make the Heavenly hookups He desires for us.

The acronym God gave me to explain how to have a Heavenly hook up was: HOOKUP

The Six Standards are:

1. Humble Yourself
2. Obey God
3. Omit sin (obstacles)
4. Keep serving
5. Understand the will of God for your life
6. Pause, Pray and Praise

2 Chronicles 7:14 says, "If my people, which are called by my name, shall humble themselves, and pray, and seek my face, and turn from their wicked ways; then will I hear from Heaven, and will forgive their sin, and will heal their land." We often think of this scripture in terms of national events, but this scripture is as personal as it is national. God operates in patterns and because of His love for us He always paves a clear path for us to live a successful Christian life.

Standard One: Humble Yourself

One of the key elements to being ready for Heavenly relationships is humility. What is humility? True humility is to understand that without God we can do nothing, but in Christ we can do all things (Phil 4:13). Humility it is truly and sincerely esteeming others more highly than oneself (Phil 2:3). Not for the purpose of getting something, but because you sincerely respect the person and are willing to submit to their needs or put their needs before your own. This is an extremely scary and potentially dangerous concept in western culture where the emphasis is return on investment in contemporary relationships. How does an individual humble him/herself in a relationship when the risk of being hurt is so high? It starts with humbling oneself before God. An individual who is humbled before God can receive God's help and inner strengthening for potential challenges as well as His insight or discernment to avoid harm (Proverbs 3:5, Proverbs 22:4, and Psalms 23).

Humility before God is knowing that you don't know and being willing to learn and do what God says do. Humility always requires an action.

• The first action is submission. Submission calls for a yielding of ones will to that of another. It is important as a Christian to have a clear definition of what God's guidelines are for relationship before entering into them. The only way to submit to the Word is to know the Word (Ps 119:105, John 8:32, II Tim 2:15).

- The second act one must take is to submit to Godly, spiritual authority is to judge the tree by its fruit. Get wisdom from people of God who are living the life. Pay attention to what they live. Not just what they say (Ps 119:104, Matt 12:33).

- The third act is to pray: to acknowledge the need for help. God said that if we ask for wisdom, He would give it to us and not chastise us for asking (Pro 4:7, Jam 1:5).

- The last act of humility is obedience in spite of fear. It takes courage to obey God (1 Sam 15:12, Jos 1:8, 9).

I remember when Bishop Coker instructed all of the single adults over the age of 24 who had completed their studies and had not been called to celibacy, to come to the alter to pray for a mate. I must confess, I did not want to go up because I was embarrassed and I was not looking for a mate at that time. However, I humbled myself and yielded to the direction of the man of God, who prayed that we would all be married within one year. I did not give much thought to the prayer once I left the church because, after all, I was not looking to get married yet. However, God answered the prophet's prayer, and in one year I was married. The whole process required an abandonment of my own wisdom as God navigated the course for my life. Humbling ourselves before God simply means that we are willing to let Him be our eyes. We have to be willing to let Him paint the picture of those with whom he would have us enter into relationships with. All too often when we are seeking a mate, we have our list written of what we want including the height, weight, hair color, skin tone, profession—even down to the kind of clothes they wear. Being humbled before God means I'm willing to see through the eyes of the Lord. When we let God show us our mate, we see the beauty He sees. The Lord shall beautify the meek with His salvation (Psalm 149:4). When you are meek, gentle, in your spirit and allow the love of God to shine through you, the radiance of the love of God will cause His glory to shine through you and regardless of what you look like or don't look like. God will cause those who are seeking Him to see your beauty and navigate your paths to the destination of His desire. Be humble before the Lord and trust that He will provide you with the companionship you need. "Better to be of a humble spirit with the lowly than to divide spoils with the rich" (Pro 16:19).

Selah 1 – Think on these Things
Humble Yourself:

1. What does God's Word say about getting married? List at least 4 things. Feel free to add others you find in the Word. (Prov.18:22, 2 Cor 6:14,Hebrews 13:4, 1 Cor 7: 9)

_____

_____

_____

_____

_____

_____

2. Based on the evidence of Godly living, who would you consider able to give you wise and Godly counsel? Try to list at least five people. (Prov 11:14, Prov 24:6, Prov 15:22, Titus 2)

_____

_____

_____

_____

_____

_____

3. Pray. Ask for Wisdom. (James 1:23)

_____

_____

_____

_____

_____

_____

_____

3a. How will you know it's God?

_____

_____

_____

_____

_____

4. If you are married, how are you demonstrating humility before God and your partner?

_____

_____

_____

5. How is your partner demonstrating humility before God and you?

_____

_____

_____

6. What counsel have you received concerning your relationship (or relationships you are pursuing)? It is often helpful to make a record of what God has shared with you lest you forget. A written record of the Spirit of God has said to you, as well as words of wisdom shared with you, will help you when circumstances become challenging.

Standard Two: Obey God

Let's take a look at this verse as it pertains to obeying God.

1 Sam 15: 3- 22: 3 Now go and smite Amalek, and utterly destroy all that they have, and spare them not; but slay man and woman, infant and suckling, ox and sheep, camel and ass. 4 And Saul gathered the people together, and numbered them in Telaim, two hundred thousand footmen, and ten thousand men of Judah.

7 And Saul smote the Amalekites from Havilah [until] thou comest to Shur, that [is] over against Egypt. 8 And he took Agag the king of the Amalekites alive, and utterly destroyed all the people with the edge of the sword. 9 But Saul and the people spared Agag, and the best of the sheep, and of the oxen, and of the fatlings, and the lambs, and all [that was] good, and would not utterly destroy them: but everything [that was] vile and refuse, that they destroyed utterly.

13 And Samuel came to Saul: and Saul said unto him, blessed [be] thou of the Lord: I have performed the commandment of the LORD. 14 And Samuel said, what [meaneth] then this bleating of the sheep in mine ears, and the lowing of the oxen which I hear? 15 And Saul said, They have brought them from the Amalekites: for the people spared the best of the sheep and of the oxen, to sacrifice unto the LORD thy God; and the rest we have utterly destroyed.

22 And Samuel said, Hath the LORD [as great] delight in burnt offerings and sacrifices, as in obeying the voice of the LORD? Behold, to obey [is] better than sacrifice, [and]

to hearken than the fat of rams. 23 For rebellion [is as] the sin of witchcraft, and stubbornness [is as] iniquity and idolatry. Because thou hast rejected the Word of the Lord, he hath also rejected thee from [being] king.

A caricature of a typical western Christian today might look something like this: picture a little boy standing in the kitchen with his hands and pockets full of cookies. The first callout reads, "Son, be obedient, you are not to take one cookie!" The response from the son reads, "Yes, ma'am, I'm being obedient, I did not take one cookie." It is common practice and human nature to behave as though instructions are only applicable if we want to follow them. We forget that all of God's instructions are purposeful and have desired outcomes that depend on our following His instructions in order to be manifested. Like Saul, we all too often find ourselves falling into the trap of delusional obedience. The instruction that God gave Saul was clear. Kill everything. Saul started the journey with good intentions to obey the Word of the Lord, however, he let "Destiny Distracters" (people, presumption, and pride) corrupt his hearing.

Let's take a closer look at a few, "Destiny Distracters":

1. People

People are placed in our lives for a reason. If you understand that you have a distinct and divine destiny then you must accept that the people you encounter on your journey have a role. It is important for us know the roles we play with the people we engage with. Saul received counsel from followers as well as from his advisors. He chose the popularity vote and followed the advice of his followers – those he was supposed to lead. When we enter into relationships with people we are either leading or following, influencing or being influenced, healing, helping or hurting. It is impossible to have an inert (non reactive) relationship. The mere meaning of the word relationship implies interaction. It is important to understand how God wants you to interact in your relationships. God is extremely interested in our relationships. While He honors our free will, His desire is for us to walk in relationships according to His design. God instructs believers not to be unequally yoked with unbelievers (2 Cor 6:14). He does not tell us to avoid unbelievers. He does tell us not to enter into a binding covenant with them. The fulfillment of our destiny is directly related to how we interact with the people in our life. We must know when to lead, follow, connect or disengage. God's instructions always supersede our opinions and the opinions of others (Romans 3: 4; Proverbs 30: 3).

2. Presumption

Presumption is predetermining or assuming one knows the intent or outcome of a matter regardless of what is stated or indicated. Saul presumed that his good intentions would supercede God's instructions. I once heard a young minister preach a sermon that instilled a principle in me that has shaped my walk with God. The principle is that good is the enemy of best. He explained that not only was good the enemy of best, but that the two concepts were diametrically opposed – opposite to each other and going in opposite directions. I came to understand that whenever an individual or society accepts doing what seems good in their own eyes, God's best, which is obedience, becomes disregarded and often despised; therefore making good the enemy of best (Hos 14:9, Act 13:10, Is 55:8). Because the standard for God's best requires a sacrifice that most are not willing to give, people generally settle for good. For example:

It is a good thing for a father to pay child support to the mother of his children.

It is best to marry and then have children and be a present and engaged father.

It is good to use condoms and protect oneself from sexually transmitted diseases.

It is best for two virgins to marry without fear of disease before having sex.

It is good that social security provides services and finances to our senior citizens.

It is best that families are prepared to care for their elderly.

In America, we have generally settled for good in a lot of things and have disregarded God's best in most things. God's best for our relationships will be revealed to us when we ask God for wisdom and obey his instructions (Jam 1:5).

Pride

Proverbs 16:18 tells us that pride goes before a fall. In I Sam 15:17, the prophet Samuel scolds King Saul, saying, "When thou [wast] little in thine own sight, [wast] thou not [made] the head of the tribes of Israel, and the LORD anointed thee king over Israel? In other words when Saul was humble, God exalted him. When he started to have success, all of a sudden he could make his own decisions about how he would follow God's instructions. Pride will cause an individual to believe their own lies. Even though God's instructions were clear, when asked by the prophet why he had disobeyed God, Saul boldly responded that he had obeyed God (just like the cookie jar). It is amazing how we try to justify our disobedience to God and get confused about why we are not blessed. God instructs us through His word and godly advisors on things to avoid, stay away from, and to even flee. I once knew a young man who wanted to marry a young lady who had just joined the church. She had just come out of a very tempestuous situation and was recovering from drug addiction. The pastor advised the couple to wait at least six months before getting married. The couple decided that since they knew it was the will God for them to be together that six months would not make a difference, so they married at the justice of the peace. Well, immediately there were problems in the relationship as they started to get to know each other. The stress of the marriage was a key driver to the young lady starting to use drugs again. By the sixth month of the marriage she was in jail for possession of narcotics. They eventually divorced. Later, the young man realized that if they had waited to marry a lot of things could have been different. The pastor wasn't saying "no" he was encouraging them to take time to prepare themselves for marriage. Pride is a deceitful thing. It presents itself as self-assurance, confidence, sacrificial, stubbornness and other attributes that cause an individual to be unable to hear wisdom or receive the truth.

Let's not be like the boy with the cookies or King Saul with the spoils. Know that God says what He means and means what He says. Let us earnestly seek the face of the Lord that we may humbly know and obey what is best.

Selah 2: Think on These Things
Obey God

1. Does the person you are with fall within the parameters of guidance provided in God's Word?
(2 Cor 6:14, Prov 23"7, Pro 31: 10)

2. If God were to ask you today have you obeyed His instructions, what would your answer be?
(Mat 15: 8, Heb 3:10)

3. List three people you spend the most time engaging with. Then consider your role in the relationship. Are you:

Leading
Following
Influencing
Being influenced
Healing
Helping
Hurting

4a. Do these relationships cause you to align with God's will for your life?

5. Have you unwittingly slipped into doing a good thing instead of the best thing? Consider one or two major decisions you need to make. Have you asked God what to do? Write down what instructions you believe you received. Do they agree with the Word of God? If so, are you doing exactly what He said?

6. What proof do you have that you are not acting out of pride? Have you submitted yourself to godly counsel?

Standard Three: Omit Sin

Generally speaking most Christians feel that they do a pretty good job of avoiding "major" sins. Usually, we consider socially unacceptable behavior as "major" sin. In regards to relationships, it is so easy to slip into sin because we tend to equate feeling good with being good. Spending time witnessing to an unbeliever is a good thing. However, if you spend time witnessing to an unbeliever that you are attracted to alone, you are opening a door for sin. As Christians, we have to flee from sin and youthful lusts. In order to avoid sin, one must make an action and conscience decision to avoid it at all cost. Romantic relationships can be very tricky. Often the romantic phase of a relationship is confused with love when it is really more of a chemical high from a naturally occurring chemical cocktail of phenyl ethylamine (PEA), dopamine and norepinephrine. This cocktail actually causes a person to feel "love sick" when he/she is not in the presence of the object of his/her affection. The chemical hormonal cocktail that is naturally emitted between two individuals is as powerful as a riptide that suddenly and relentlessly sweeps people into its path and pulls them under. After the couple has been dating for 18-24 months the chemicals have usually receded to a normal level, allowing each of the individuals to see each other more realistically. Unfortunately, by that time, many have made major life decisions like having sex, having a baby, or getting married. The key point here is to be mindful not to confuse feelings with the fact. Using the Word of God and Godly standards as your guide is the only way to avoid entering into sin. The entrance of sin is subtle. The book of Proverbs is full of warnings regarding sin's craftiness and lure. The challenge we have is choosing to refuse seasons of pleasure to gain a lifetime of blessings. James 4:17 says, "Therefore to him that knoweth to do good, and doeth [it] not, to him it is sin." Sin is always at the door luring us at our weakest moments to let it have rule over our lives. One of the primary tricks of the devil is to cause us to feel like we are alone in our decision-making. Receiving and following Godly counsel will help you to omit sin. Proverbs 14:14 says, "The backslider in heart shall be filled with his own ways."

Receiving input from other people can help us avoid mistakes when it comes to relationships. Other people can see dangerous patterns in your relationship that you may not be able to see because you are under the influence. However, if you make it clear to others that you don't really want to hear what they have to say, most people will say nothing, to maintain their friendship with you. The key to getting input from others is actually receiving the input others give you.

During the decision making process of marriage for DeWayne and I, we submitted to four pastors who knew us as well as godly family members. They asked us important questions about our relationship and took time to ensure we understood what the concept of oneness was about.

Even in decisions regarding partnering in business transactions it is important to have counsel. The Bible tells us in Proverbs 11:14, "Where no counsel [is], the people fall: but in the multitude of counselors [there is] safety." Proverbs 15: 22 says, "Without counsel purposes are disappointed: but in the multitude of counselors they are established." Proverbs 24:6 says, "For by wise counsel thou shalt make thy war: and in multitude of counselors [there is] safety."

Another key step to avoiding sin is to know yourself. All too often we commit sin because we do not look bluntly into the mirror and acknowledge the areas where we are weak. Even if we do know where we are weak, we try to overcome the weakness by ourselves. We are made for relationships. That means that we need other people to survive. We need someone to help us be strong. We need someone to agree with us and let us know that we can make it. Placing yourself in a supportive environment with nurturing and inspirational people will help you omit sin. One practice that will help you stand strong and omit sin from your life is accountability. Whenever you are about to take an action that might bring you into an area of temptation, tell a spiritually mature friend exactly what you are about to do, or better yet ask their opinion regarding your plans. If you are not comfortable with just discussing your plans with a mature Christian, that should be a good indicator or red flag that you are probably about to make a mistake. Sin loves darkness.

Selah 3 - Think on These Things
Omit Sin

1. Are there things in your life that the Holy Spirit is prompting you to let go of? What are they?

2. What do your spiritual counselors have to say about your current attitude, actions and associations?

3. Have you completely submitted to God as Lord, complete ruler, over your life?

4. We know that change is hard. In order to gain victory in your life. Make a plan of action and ask God for help in finding someone to keep you accountable.

   a. What one action will you do every day for the next 40 days?

   b. What one action will you cease for the next 40 days?

   c. What one scripture will you stand on to help you walk in victory?

Standard Four: Keep Serving

There are many scriptures that instruct us on the serving God with patience and joy. The Weymouth New Testament writes the words of Jesus found in Luke 21:19. It says, "By your patient endurance you will purchase your lives." Neh 8: 10 says, "The joy of the Lord is your strength." Ps 100:2 says, "Serve the LORD with gladness: come before his presence with singing." There are several scriptures that instruct the people of God to stand still and wait on God (Ex 14:13; Is 40: 3, Ps27:13; and Eph 6:13).

A good habit to practice while we are waiting on the Lord is to keep doing the fundamental things of our salvation. Keep reading, studying, praying, and witnessing for Jesus. As he was walking down the hot humid streets of Biloxi, Mississippi, DeWayne kept the eager pace of evangelism high. Waiting for God to manifest his promise of a seven fold return on all that the devil had stolen from him, waiting for the manifestation of a not only restored but a magnified household, he was determined to stand on the promises of God. Determined to stand on the word God had spoken to his heart. Believing what Jeremiah 1:12 said, "God watches over his word to perform it..." When we are waiting for clarity regarding God's will in our life it is easy to start creating our own answers. It is imperative that we receive the written (Logos) and spoken (Rhema) Word of God. The Rhema word of God is a word that is a living, now, revealed word of God. The written word is the solid foundation upon which we stand.

Why is standing so important? Because God is a God of timing. Remember that in order to be in a relationship there must be more than one person involved. That means that God may have to move in several lives to effect the necessary change in yours. If you remember how God had to move to provide a financial hookup, aka deliverance, in DeWayne's life, let us consider the three other hearts that had to be touched, consider the physical placement of people in the right place at the right time. The cashier, the regional director and the bank president. By trusting God to do what He does and not trying to fix things himself, DeWayne was able to see the goodness of the Lord. It is great to know that God is interested in every aspect of our lives; the challenge is standing still and letting God fight our battles. Eph 6:12 reminds us, "For we wrestle not against flesh and blood, but against principalities, against powers, against the rulers of the darkness of this world, against spiritual wickedness in high [places]." Verse 13 says, "Wherefore take unto you the whole armor of God that ye may be able to withstand in the evil day, and having done all, to stand."

Selah 4 – Think on These Things

Keep Serving

1. How is your stance? Are you standing with an open heart for whatever God does or are you trying to manage how God works deliverance in your life?

2. Do you remember what God promised you? Have you written it down so you will not forget?

3. Stand against the major enemies of your faith: fear, doubt, and impatience.
    a. Fear says it looks impossible. Faith says we walk by faith not by sight. 2 Cor 5:7.
    b. Doubt says you can't do it. Faith says with God all things are possible. Matthew 19:26.
    c. Impatience says give up. Luke 21:19 says in patience possess you your souls. Therefore my beloved, having done all to stand, stand. Ephesians 6:13.

Standard Five: Understand the will of God for your life

It is extremely important for us to know that God has a purpose for us and for us to discover what the will of God is concerning our lives. When we understand what it is that God intends for us to do, we are more likely to find ourselves on a path that will lead us in the right direction. Each person has to make a choice as we approach this point in our lives. We must decide that whatever the Lord presents to us as our purpose we will obey and serve with gladness. Far too often, I hear individuals decide to wait until the right partner comes along to seek God's will for their lives. The development of God's gifts in you, happen throughout your life (Your pathway does not begin when you meet your partner; it is supposed to be lived out every day of your life.). To try to wait until you feel complete is paradox. Whether you have you have a partner or not, your completion comes when you are walking in the will of God. So how does one get to that point? The first step is to seek God's counsel. Simply ask God, what is my purpose? What am I supposed to be doing right now to operate in my purpose? Jam 1: 5 says, "If any of you lack wisdom, let him ask of God, that giveth to all [men] liberally, and does not find fault; and it shall be given him."

The next step is to associate yourself with someone who is doing what you believe you are called to do and be a disciple. For this to take place, you must submit yourself to discipleship. Be a part of a church that prays for its singles to hear from God concerning their destiny and their God chosen mate. As we have said, God will be as intimately involved in your relationships as you allow Him to be.

Col 1:9-10. For this cause we also, since the day we heard [it], do not cease to pray for you, and to desire that ye might be filled with the knowledge of his will in all wisdom and spiritual understanding; That ye might walk worthy of the Lord unto all pleasing, being fruitful in every good work, and increasing in the knowledge of God.

Jer 1: 5. Before I formed thee in the belly I knew thee; and before thou camest forth out of the womb I sanctified thee, [and] I ordained thee a prophet unto the nations.

Mat 6: 33. But seek ye first the kingdom of God, and his righteousness; and all these things shall be added unto you.

Additional Reading: Ephesians Chapter 1. Focus on verses 8-11.

Selah 5 – Think on These Things

Understand the Will of God for You

1.   A formula for discovering your purpose: Answer the questions below and based on your answers seek God on how to use who he made you for His glory.

a.   What is your passion? (If you are always coming up with ideas on how to help fix problems or breach gaps in this area it may be your passion.)

b.   What are your talents? (Naturally occurring abilities. We often take our talents for granted and may need input from others to see them)

c.   What are your gifts? (God given abilities, insights and sensitivities used especially to serve others)

d.   What is your physique (What are you physically, mentally, and emotionally able to do? God is able to supernaturally empower you if it is His will.)

e.   What are your skills (You may have to sharpen your skills to walk in your purpose)

Look at your answers and ask God how you can these things work together to glorify God.

My answers: passion: relationships; talents: organizing events; gifts: service, leadership and teaching; physique: a soothing voice, can stand and walk for long periods of time; skills: counseling, training. Purpose: provided relationship skills to the body of Christ.

I admit, through the years I have had my share of discussions with God about what I really wanted to do, which was sing and play an instrument. While I can hold a note and harmonize fairly well, I am absolutely no lead singer. And though I have made many attempts at learning to play an instrument, it is the hardest thing in the world for me to do. Therefore, I stopped frustrating myself and the grace of God and walked in the doors of my life that were open. Those doors led to training. I must confess, while my heart feels just a twitch of envy and amazement when I watch singers effortlessly belt out notes that make you want to stand up and sit down at the same time, I am thankful to know that God knows my frame and that whatever He does in my life is for my good.

Standard Six: Pause to Pray and Praise

This last step is critical. When emotions are running high and we want an answer yesterday, one the hardest thing to do is to just wait. That's why I like the word pause. To pause means to choose to stop. Not by force from any outside influence, but by your own will you choose to demonstrate faith in God. Having done all to stand; we stand (Eph 6:13). When we pause we take dominion over time, our emotions and bring our thoughts into submission to the Word of God. In other words, we Selah, Selah means to consider the whole matter and meditate on what the Word instructs us concerning it. Prov 18:13, "He that answereth a matter before he heareth [it], its [is] folly and shame unto him."

Pausing is exercise that allows you to grow in spiritual maturity. It is an opportunity to discover what is really in your heart. This is an opportunity that God provides to test what you have learned in His word and it should not be missed but rather cherished. The Father knows what is in you and before you and desires you to have complete victory through the Word of God over every seen and unseen obstacle in your life. Luke 21:19 tells us that in your patience we possess (rule) our souls (mind, will, and emotions).

While you are pausing and considering the Word, you are also praying that you might be strengthened in the inner man. Since your focus is that you may be made complete in Christ. Then your prayers should definitely be for God to help you be ready for any and all of the hook ups He has in store for you. Too often our eyes are blinded by the urgency of situations and we miss Holy Ghost appointments that result in our having to re-accomplish the test. Rest assured however, if you failed the first, second or last opportunity that God provided, He will complete what He started in you. Psalm 138:8 "The LORD will fulfill [his purpose] for me; your love, O LORD, endures forever--do not abandon the works of your hands." Each of the actions that God gave us in this instructional manual will require much prayer to execute successfully. It will take much prayer to be humble, to omit sin, to obey God, to keep serving and to understand the will of God concerning you. Phi 1:6, "Being confident of this that he who began a good work in you will carry it on to completion until the day of Christ Jesus."

Know that when you pray you have what you asked for: Mark 11:24, "Therefore I say unto you, what things you so ever desire, when ye pray, believe that ye receive them, and ye shall have them." If you do not know what to pray use the Lord's Prayer found at Mark 6:9. When you settle yourself in the Lord and commit to trusting Him, you can then praise God for the manifestation of promises not yet seen. Faith filled praise is an invitation for God to come into your presence.

- Psalm 22:33 says: But thou [art] holy, [O thou] that inhabits the praises of Israel. God will dwell in the praises of His people.
- Psalm 63:4, I will praise you as long as I live, and in your name I will lift up my hands.
- Psalm 147:1, Praise you the LORD: for it is good to sing praises unto our God; for it is pleasant; and praise is comely.

• Psalm 33:1, Rejoice in the LORD, O you righteous: for praise is comely for the upright.

Selah 6 – Think on These Things

Pause, Pray and Praise (PP&P)

1. Has your current situation become a constant frustration? Perhaps it's time to PP&P.

2. If this situation looks very familiar, perhaps it's time to pause, just in-case this is a re-test. This time make sure you move in God only.

3. Pray and say only what the Word of God says about you and your situation. Remember He watches over His Word.

4. Whatever you do. DON'T STOP PRAISING GOD!

God Bless You.

Sis Jacqui

Reference: All scripture references are taken from the King James Version of the Holy Bible.

www.ingramcontent.com/pod-product-compliance
Lightning Source LLC
Chambersburg PA
CBHW050125280326
41933CB00010B/1247